# Hello, New You!

Transform Your Life and Fulfill Your Destiny

By Erin Weisbrodt

*Hello, New You!: Transform Your Life and Fulfill Your Destiny*
Copyright © 2023 by Erin Weisbrodt

All rights reserved. This book or parts thereof may not be reproduced in any form, stored in a retrieval system, or transmitted in any form by any means electronic, mechanical, photocopy, recording, or otherwise without prior written permission of the publisher, except as provided by United States of America copyright law.

Cover design: Rigel Drake-Garcia
Editor: Erin Weisbrodt

Unless otherwise noted, Scripture quotations are taken from the New Living Translation (NLT) of the Holy Bible. Public Domain.

Other Scripture quotations have been taken from the following translations: Amplified Bible (AMP), Amplified Classic Bible (AMPC), English Standard Version (ESV), King James Version (KJV), New American Standard Bible (NASB; NASB95), New English Translation (NET), New International Version (NIV), New King James Version (NKJV), New Living Translation (NLT), The Passion Translation (TPT), and Young's Literal Translation (YLT). Full copyright information is found at the end of this book.

Bolding within Scripture quotations was added by the author; brackets added are indicated.

Author contact: Erin Weisbrodt
www.NewYouMinistries.com

Cataloging-in-Publication Data is on file with the Library of Congress. Library of Congress Control Number: 2023951718

ISBN 979-8-9892799-0-6 (Softcover)

10 9 8 7 6 5 4 3 2 1
1st edition, December 2023
Printed in the United States of America

# Dedication

Precious Lord, thank You! I would not be here without You. I have loved encountering You every day, and the power of Jesus' great sacrifice in my life. Father, Son, and Holy Spirit, You are my Everything.

To My Husband, Greg, I adore you with all of my heart and look up to you every day of my life. Thank you for showing me the love of Christ.

To My Loving Family: I am so grateful that you loved me and gave me so many second chances. Thank you for never giving up on me. I wouldn't be here without you.

# Contents

Dedication .................................................................................................. i
Introduction ............................................................................................. v
1  God Is Love ........................................................................................ 1
2  Living in Your New Identity ............................................................ 17
3  Born Again Power ........................................................................... 45
4  The Power of the Word .................................................................. 65
5  Is Your Mind a Bully? ..................................................................... 93
6  Your Heart Matters ....................................................................... 109
7  A Relationship of Trust ................................................................. 135
8  A Life of Purpose .......................................................................... 157
9  The Power of Daily Commitment ................................................ 183
10  Strong in Faith ............................................................................. 199
11  Ruled by the Spirit ...................................................................... 235
12  Results That Last a Lifetime! ..................................................... 275
Seeking a Christ-Centered Community? ......................................... 307
Appendix A Receiving Jesus ............................................................. 309
Appendix B Receiving the Holy Spirit ............................................. 311
Endnotes ............................................................................................ 313
Additional Copyrights ....................................................................... 317
Help Share God-Given Messages around the World! ..................... 319
About the Author .............................................................................. 321

# Introduction

What does *life transformation* mean to you? If there is one area of your life where you would like to see transformation, what would it be? Maybe it's hard for you to think of one thing, or maybe you can think of several. I've experienced transformation in every area of my life. I'd like to tell you how.

As a 15-year-old, I became a drug addict. After seven years of masking my internal pain with drugs, sex, alcohol, self-mutilation, and self-prescribed medications, my life was a disaster. Any hope for restoration was nowhere in sight, so instead, I tried to take my own life. Thankfully, I failed. After a couple more bouts of sobriety followed by intoxication, I hit rock bottom. I thought my life and any possibility of good in my life was completely over.

You can imagine my shock when my family surprised me with an intervention. I remember to this day, being in a strange living room with eight family members and a professional interventionist sitting in a circle. They told me how much they loved me and how worried they were for my life. Even though I was shocked and numb towards it all, their love and forgiveness towards me filled me with hope. Since I didn't have hope for myself, I stood on their hope for quite some time.

Several weeks later, I rededicated my faith and my life to Jesus Christ. Every ounce of strength that I had went to my faith and to recovering all that was lost in my life. I sought the truth about God (the Father, the Son Jesus Christ, and the Holy Spirit). I read the Bible diligently each day. In my attempt to find God, I discovered freedom from all my disabilities and disorders. I encountered God as a real person, in whom I could have an intimate relationship with each day—where I found help, comfort, inner peace, and provision for every need I experience in life. From my relationship with God, I not only found restoration and redemption from my past, but I uncovered a future, a hope, and a purpose for my life.

This would be my definition of transformation. *Transformation* is a change for good in your life that causes you to want to get out of bed in the morning and look forward to the day ahead. That may sound simple, but for me, it was radical and revolutionary.

In the Bible, transformation refers to being changed into an entirely different creation. Like a caterpillar transforming into a butterfly.

Did you know that your life can transform so much, that you don't even recognize *the old you* because *the new you* is so brilliant?

God, in His Word (the Bible), has laid out a blueprint that we can follow to help us walk out this transformation in our life. I like to call it, learning how to live in your new identity in Christ. It's simple, and anyone can do it. All it requires is a believing heart. With an open heart, God will lead you to transformation in every area of your life, just like He did for me. It's as simple as getting dressed in the morning—taking off your old self, and putting on your new self (Col. 3:9-10)!

If you don't know this yet, God loves you and has good plans for you. When you believe this and are living in a close relationship with God, everything else in your life will be accomplished by God's grace. God's grace is His strength in your weakness; His divine ability, favor, and provision working in your life. You can't always see it with your natural eyes, but God is working behind the scenes to bring forth His perfect plans for your life. Trust me, His plans for you are far better than anything you could ask for or dream of. No matter what choices you've made or continue to make, God's purpose for your life is still intact, dear one, and His grace is bringing it to pass.

The principles laid out in this book helped me to replace old destructive behaviors and thought patterns with new, life-giving behaviors. I received strength to do these things through my new identity in Christ. If there have been some old behaviors, negative thought patterns, or situations in your life that have been hard to overcome, those things are about to become possible in Christ. Let me encourage you to take your time with the truths in this book. During your study time with the Lord, look up each scripture on your own, and let God speak to your heart regarding these things. After each chapter, there is a dedicated "Moment of Reflection" to help you do this. I am only scratching the surface on these topics, and there is so much more that you can discover on your own.

If you have made Jesus Christ your Lord and Savior, then you can do these things too! If you haven't made Jesus your Lord, don't worry, you can do so now. Turn to Appendix A so I can walk you through this process. When you get born again, you are no longer powerless, hopeless, and helpless. In Christ, you are filled with power, purpose, and strength to walk in *your new identity* and to fulfill God's awesome plans for your life!

Let me ask you again. How would you like to see your life transformed? In what areas would you like to see a change for good? Feel free to write these down so that you can review them and measure your growth in a short span of time. Then, ask God to help you transform these areas through the principles in His Word and in this book.

I'm privileged to walk with you through this journey of transformation as you live in your new identity in Christ!

> Forget the former things; do not dwell on the past. See, I am doing a new thing! Now it springs up; do you not perceive it? I am making a way in the wilderness and streams in the wasteland.
> (Isaiah 43:18-19 NIV)

# Chapter 1

## God Is Love

### God's Love Leads to a Life of Transformation

*...God is love. [He is the originator of love, and it is an enduring attribute of His nature.]*
—1 John 4:8 AMP

After seven years of drug addiction, I rededicated my life to God, and I decided that I truly wanted to live for Him. I finally came to a place of surrender. My heart was set on pleasing Him and getting to know Him better. Because of my newfound dedication, it seemed logical to start reading my Bible every day so I could get to know God more. However, I must say, the Bible was pretty hard for me to understand. It seemed like He was a harsh God sometimes, and a loving God at other times. Even though I didn't understand the Bible perfectly, I felt compelled to continue my pursuit. I continued to read the Bible despite my lack of understanding. Then, I found a Bible teacher, which helped me to understand God's true nature and that He is a loving, kind, merciful, forgiving God; that God created me for relationship with Him, and to accomplish a specific purpose on this earth. This truly changed the way that I related to God. Instead of working to earn His love and affection, I just rested and received His love. This also transformed the way that I spent my time with Him each day. Instead of entering into His presence begging for forgiveness—afraid that He would strike me down for the sin of my past and present—I entered into His presence with praise, thanksgiving, and an expectation to receive something good from Him. This helped me to hear God's voice and direction more clearly, and I was able to understand the Bible in a completely different way. I actually *wanted* to read the Bible and be in a relationship with God. God is cool!

Through this new relationship and understanding, I encountered the heart and will of God for my life—that He had a plan, a purpose, and a destiny for me! Then, I discovered that His love, goodness, and purpose for my life were not limited to me alone. God offers this loving redemption for anyone who's willing to seek Him.

## Who Is God?

In order to have a personal, intimate relationship with God (which is the most important thing on earth), you need to know who He is. Understanding who God is will help you to understand the Bible and divide truth from error. Why is it important to know the truth? Because in the world today, there are a lot of lies and very little truth being told.

Throughout the Bible, scripture warns us to know the truth so that you can live in freedom, free from bondage. If you cannot discern the truth of God from the lies of the world, then you will not walk in the freedom Jesus paid for you to have. When you live your life by the truths in God's Word, you will live a life of transformation. The truth about God can be discovered in the Bible.

> **When you live your life by the truths in God's Word, you will live a life of transformation.**

Sanctify them in the truth [set them apart for Your purposes, make them holy]; **Your word is truth.** (John 17:17 AMP)

For a long time, I thought that I needed to earn God's love and approval. I thought that He was mad at me. I thought that He was in control of everything that happened in the earth. None of those things are true. I'm so glad that I took the time to *seek the truth*, because I discovered that God is not who other people had painted Him to be. God is loving, kind, powerful, always with you, gentle, strong, giving, forgiving, merciful, gracious, faithful. The list of God's virtues and character traits could go on forever. In fact, we will spend all of eternity discovering the vastness of God's goodness, kindness, and love for us, and we will praise Him and glorify Him for all eternity. That's how good God is! One of the most important things I learned about God is that His character and nature always coincide with love. This means that *God is only good, and He never causes bad things to happen.* Bad things happen because sin entered the world and people have free will. God doesn't cause sickness and storms and death. That is all the result of sin. God is the Author of life, creation, and every good and perfect gift comes from Him (James 1:17). With these truths in mind, it helped me to better understand who God is, which helped me to correctly interpret the Bible, and divide truth from error.

Instead of taking everything that people say at face value, I began to seek the truth for myself, and I encourage you to do the same. To help you get started, I would like to cover three key points about the love of God. These points will set you on a firm foundation, so that you can understand God, and relate to Him according to the truth of the Bible.

> **One of the most important things I learned about God is that His character and nature always coincide with love.**

Key #1: God is love. First John 4:7-8 says, "Dear friends, let us continue to love one another, for love comes from God. Anyone who loves is a child of God and knows God. But anyone who does not love does not know God, for God is love." If God is love, then God is only good, and He is the Author of all that is good. God does not cause bad things to happen.

Key #2: God's love is a gift. Ephesians 2:8 says, "God saved you by his grace when you believed. And you can't take credit for this; it is a gift from God." Your performance is never a factor in your relationship with God. Your positive efforts (and negative efforts) cannot and will not change God's love for you.

Key #3: God's love is kind. Titus 3:4-5 says, "...When God our Savior revealed his kindness and love, he saved us, not because of the righteous things we had done, but because of his mercy. He washed away our sins, giving us a new birth and new life through the Holy Spirit." No matter what you have done, no matter how many times you have done it, God looks at you with eyes of pure love, joy, and kindness. God isn't angry with you—He's pleased with you!

## Relationship with God

Knowing that God loves you and that He's not mad at you makes it a lot easier to seek Him, doesn't it? Let me say it this way. Why would I want to spend time with someone who's mad at me, who's always unhappy with my choices, or who's constantly judging me? I wouldn't want to spend time with that person! I definitely wouldn't be in a relationship with someone who causes bad things to happen in my life. Knowing that *God loves you,* that your choices don't change God's love for you, and that He's always looking at you with eyes of loving kindness changes things, doesn't it?

When I discovered the truth about God's love towards me, it made me want to know Him even more. Every day, I learn a new facet of God's love, goodness, and faithfulness in my life. I have learned that God is always waiting for my invitation to Him. He never forces me to spend time with Him, but when I make time to be with Him, *He is always there,* drawing me further and deeper into His loving heart, and revealing a relationship with Him that, for a long time, I didn't know existed. Now that I know the truth, I will never turn back from Him. I have experienced God as my Father, Brother, Lover, Friend, Teacher, Counsellor, Healer, Provider, Protector, Defender, Comforter, and my Helper. God is power, wisdom, and strength in my life that I never had before. And it all stems from a loving relationship with Him—a correct understanding of who He truly this. This relationship with God is available to anyone and everyone on this earth, thanks to faith in Jesus Christ, the Son of God.

Your relationship with God is the most important thing in this lifetime. If you want to live a happy, healthy, successful life, then awake each day with the intention of getting to know Him more. Get up in the morning with God on your mind and live to know Him until you rest your head at night. This will fill your days with more joy than anything on this earth can offer, and it will prosper you in everything you do. God is so blessed when His children take time to be with Him and seek to know Him more. When you do this, God blesses you in return and tries to find ways to bless you more!! Blessings overtake you and success will overcome you, just because you know the Author of life itself. Spending time with God will fill you with wisdom and understanding that surpasses any wealth the world could tempt you with. Relationship with God is the most satisfying and fulfilling thing that you could pursue in this lifetime.

## A Firm Foundation

These simple truths from God's Word will help you to live with a right understanding of God's heart for you. For example, if I believe that God is displeased with me, that He causes me to be sick and poor, or that His love is conditional based on my good works, then I will live with an unhealthy, untrue perspective on God. Those toxic beliefs will be cracks in my mental reasoning and will limit my progress on this earth because I'm not living in the freedom that Jesus paid for. Jesus paid for every person's sin, so they could be forgiven and have intimacy with God; to live each day in peace, prosperity, joy, complete healing and wholeness, and financial wealth and security. I will be unable to experience these things and fulfill my life's purpose if I'm unable to discern good from evil on this earth—truth versus error. This will prohibit me from growing and moving forward with God, and it will prohibit me from excelling in life.

Until I understood the truth about God and His love for me, I was stuck in life, and I was dragged through vicious cycles of defeat and destructive behavior. Like my story, if you don't know how much God loves you and that His will toward you is good, then you'll question Him, and you won't rely on Him for everything you need. To make sure that you are getting the most out of your precious faith in Christ, living in complete freedom, and experiencing the transformation that Jesus paid for, then you need to have a proper understanding of who God is.

> **If you don't know how much God loves you and that His will toward you is good, then you'll question Him, and you won't rely on Him for everything you need.**

When you know who God is and how much He loves you, then you will live the victorious Christian life *in your new identity.*

## These Truths Changed My Life

Even as a drug addict, I loved God. But I didn't have a right understanding of God, or how to apply the Bible to my life. Yes, I was a Christian, but my life was unchanged. I loved God, I read the Bible, and my heart was in the right place, but I caused so much destruction by the way I lived my life.

In hindsight, I realized that just because you believe something, doesn't mean you're going to experience the fullness of it. What I mean is, just because I believed in God and loved God before this time, doesn't mean that I was experiencing the fullness of life that His Word promised me. Before I encountered the truth of God's love and His transforming power, I still believed in God and loved God, but my life was powerless and unchanged. I was stuck—hopeless and helpless and a victim to all the troubles that life offers. I was stuck in cycles of destructive behavior like addiction, immoral relationships, sin, eating disorders, poor self-image, anxiety, depression, suicidal thoughts, and social anxiety around others. Can you relate to any of these things? Maybe you can, or maybe you can't, but if you can, then you don't have to stay there. There is hope and there is freedom for you! When I determined to seek God and discover who He is, I discovered a life free from these bondages and full of transformation.

To experience the fullness of God in our lifetime, we must participate with Him. God is waiting on an invitation from each person, and a heart that is ready to seek Him and discover the truth about who He is. We discover the truth about God through His Word and Spirit. The Word is a firm foundation that the believer can build their life upon, and the Holy Spirit is the One who draws us to Jesus and leads us into all truth. Together, those three things make up God Himself. God is the Father, the Son Jesus Christ (the Word), and the Holy Spirit. We need all three in order to live life in unity with God. Understanding these things will help you to cooperate with God and invite Him to lovingly lead you into all truth.

Remember, I loved God and had good intentions towards Him in my heart, but I needed to know the truth that would continue to set me free.

Jesus said to the people who believed in him, "You are truly my disciples if you remain faithful to my teachings. **And you will know the truth, and the truth will set you free."** (John 8:31-32)

The truth is the only thing that can lead you to a life of freedom. Freedom is where you truly discover the depths of God's love for you. God's love for you contains the power to remove anything from your life that is holding you prisoner. God's love for you is where you encounter a relationship with God that is out of this world—literally. Relationship with God is where you enter into a life that is too good to be true. *From this place of understanding God's love,* you can live a transformed life, walking in your new identity as a Christian, and Holy Spirit will lead you into every other truth that you need to succeed, thrive, and flourish in life. This is the life that God intended you to live all along. He is ready, willing, and excited to reveal Himself to you and guide you to your best possible life ever: a life of passion, purpose, and power.

# Surrender

Take a moment and ask yourself, "Where am I today? What am I willing to give to God?" God is here with you right now. He's meeting you right where you are, with whatever you're willing to give to Him.

Wherever you stand today, I want you to know that God is not offended by your stance. He loves you perfectly, unconditionally, and intimately. His eyes are on you. He sees *all of you*. He isn't looking at your past or at your sin. He is only looking at you—fixed on you with perfect, warm, healing love. God is constantly healing your past, comforting your present, and restoring your soul. So, wherever you are today, come to Him. God wants you to come to Him in whatever state you're in, with whatever you're willing to give to Him. God isn't asking you to be perfect or to clean up your life. Just come. Come. He will meet you where you are, and He wants to help you, love you, and be in a relationship *with you right now*. Don't wait any longer.

In the beginning, that's all that I did. I opened my heart to Him and gave Him the little bit that I had to offer. I had nothing to give God...my life was completely ruined. I had committed every sin in the Bible. I was completely bankrupt in every way; I was filthy inside out. I didn't make a huge commitment—I just did what I could with where I was. Hopeless and helpless, I gave Him my heart—that's the only thing that I had to give to Him.

Trust me, if you open your heart to God today, He will do the rest. Jesus will clean you, restore you, and redeem every area of your life.

If you're ready, then let's make a faith commitment now to turn your life over to Him. Whether you're a new Christian, or undecided and still seeking the truth, or if you have been walking with the Lord for some time, remind yourself once again of how you want to see God transform your life. Allow yourself to let go of how you viewed God in the past and start with a clean slate today. Ask Him to show you the truth about who He is and how much He loves you.

If you feel comfortable, take a moment to write your faith commitment in the space provided. I included an example of my faith commitment if you need help. I believe that you'll experience supernatural transformation through the power of His love as you read this book.

## *My Faith Commitment:*

_____

_____

_____

_____

_____

_____

## *An Example of Erin's Faith Commitment:*

*Dear God, thank You for loving me, forgiving me, and showing me the truth about who You are. I believe in You and trust that You're good, even if I don't have all the answers. Reveal yourself to me, so I can discover Your goodness and know the truth. I ask for wisdom, courage, and strength to seek the truth and find it. Help me to always have an open heart before You, and to love You with all my strength. I don't know what's best for my life, but*

*You do, so I surrender every area of my life to You today, and ask You, Holy Spirit, to lead me into all truth. In Jesus' name. Amen.*

# Chapter 2

# Living in Your New Identity

Embracing the Person God Made You to Be

*Therefore if anyone is in Christ [that is, grafted in, joined to Him by faith in Him as Savior], he is a new creature [reborn and renewed by the Holy Spirit]; the old things [the previous moral and spiritual condition] have passed away. Behold, new things have come [because spiritual awakening brings a new life].*
—2 Corinthians 5:17 AMP

Once I discovered how much God loved me, it transformed my relationship with Him. I began to see Him, others, and the rest of the world in a new light. I thought to myself, *if God loves me this much, then He must love everyone this much!* It transformed the lens through which I saw this beautiful world. It also changed the way I viewed myself. As a drug addict, I hated myself. The decisions I had made for so long caused me to walk with my eyes cast down—a reflection of the state of my heart. I don't know if you can relate to this, but I felt hopeless and helpless. My future looked gray and grim from where I stood, but God continued to speak hope to my heart. Spending time in His Word was changing the way that I thought. I noticed that I started making better decisions for myself—decisions that added value and blessing and virtue to my life, instead of decisions that harmed myself and others, which *used to be my norm.*

From my relationship with God, I began to recognize myself through *my new identity in Christ,* instead of the lens of my past. Experiencing the unconditional love of God taught me that God wasn't judging me all the time like I thought He was. Instead, God was looking at me with eyes of pure love, satisfaction, and pleasure. I was completely forgiven, redeemed, and made new in Christ. I was no longer the sum of my past!

This insight about my born-again state led to an entirely new understanding: even though my body and my emotions were a part of me, they were not the *true me*. I am a completely new creature because my spirit is brand new in Christ! This truth filled me with resurrection power and strength to keep pressing on in life. No matter how hard it seemed at times, my relationship with God gave me courage, hope, and boldness to rely on the truth, instead of focusing on the difficulty of the present. This truth took me from a victim mindset to a life-overcoming victor. It enabled me to take responsibility for my life and empowered me to make wise decisions, which turned the ashes of my past into something beautiful.

## A Triune Being

The Bible says that you are made up of three parts: spirit, soul, and body.

Now may the God of peace himself make you completely holy and may **your spirit and soul and body** be kept entirely blameless at the coming of our Lord Jesus Christ. (1 Thessalonians 5:23 NET)

I see from this verse that God is interested in your whole being, and that whole being is made up of a spirit, a soul, and a body. Some people break this down by saying you are a spirit, you have a soul, and you live in a body. Without a spirit, you would have no life. Without a soul, you would have no emotions, thoughts, or free will. Without a body, you would not have a house for your spirit and your soul. You need a body to live in this world. In heaven, your body will pass away, and your spirit will live on.

This verse also says that God wants you to be complete, holy, entire, and to be blameless when Jesus comes back. Jesus is coming back to this earth to take those who believe in Him with Him into eternal life, and God wants you to be ready for Him when He comes. God isn't interested in leaving you where you are. He wants to elevate your life and bring you higher! God wants to transform your life from the inside out, and all of this starts in your spirit. He makes your spirit complete, brand new, and born again through believing in Jesus. When you believe in Jesus Christ as the Son of God and confess Him as the Lord and Savior of your life, then you receive His perfect, holy, sinless Spirit inside of your spirit. Your old, sinful nature passes away, and you receive Jesus' nature inside of you. You are no longer a sinner; you are a saint! You are brand new in the truest part of who you are—your spirit—which will live on for all of eternity. Nothing can change this part of you—not your actions, and not someone else's actions or opinion of you. You are perfect, pure, true, holy, and spotless in your inner self. This is what it means to be "born again."

From your spiritual new birth, God is able to bless, sanctify, and purify your whole being (your soul and your body). You can draw out the life of Christ that's in your born-again spirit, into your soul, and then into your body, which then overflows into every area of your life. This is how every part of you and your life can be set aside for the purpose and glory of God. When your spirit, soul, and body are aligned with God, your life becomes transformed into the image and original plan God had for your life.

> **When your spirit, soul, and body are aligned with God, your life becomes transformed into the image and original plan God had for your life.**

Let's look at some definitions of the words in 1 Thessalonians 5:23. [1]The word *spirit* in Greek means the vital principal by which the body is animated; your breath, or life. As I mentioned earlier, your spirit is the part of you that will live on after this life. When you become born again, your spirit becomes brand new.

Since God is a Spirit, this is how God sees you and relates to you—in the spirit. Because Jesus paid for all of your sins on the cross, you are able to go to God sinless, spotless, and blameless in your spirit. You have the spirit of Jesus Christ inside of you.

The next word is soul. [2]In Greek, the word *soul* means the residence of the feelings, desires, affections, aversions, and your heart. The soul is commonly made up of the mind, will, and emotions. Every area of life including health, finances, and relationships, suffer when the soul is not healthy and prospering. Third John 2 says, "Beloved, I pray that you may prosper in all things and be in health, just as your soul prospers." [3]The words *may prosper* mean to grant a prosperous journey, to help on the way, succeed in reaching, to lead by a direct and easy way; to grant a successful issue, to cause to prosper; to prosper, and to be successful.

A prospering soul leads your entire life's journey to success. Many things come into consideration when it comes to soul prosperity like emotional health, spiritual maturity, healthy relationships, mental health, a safe home life, and so on.

Your soul also contains your heart, which is where the spirit and soul unite. In the Bible, the heart is referred to as being part of the spirit (Ps. 51:10) and the soul (Ps. 24:4).

The heart is also described as your inner self (1 Sam. 16:7, 2 Cor. 4:16).

Your soul is your character and personality. This is shaped over the expanse of your life and can change through experience and conviction. You can even choose who you want to be in your soul, because God gave you the freedom of will-power or free will, which you can use for good, for evil, or to straddle the two.

[4]Lastly, the word *body* means the living body. This is the vessel that you get to live in on this earth. The Bible says that you are fearfully and wonderfully made (Ps. 139:14), and that you are created in the image of God (Gen. 1:26-27). You are a steward of this body, just as you are a steward of the promises, talents, and abilities that God has given you. When you get born again, your spirit becomes identical to Jesus' Spirit, but your soul and body stay the same. That's why God instructs you to renew your mind by reading the Word of God (Rom. 12:2), so that your life can be transformed into the image of Jesus Christ.

Just because we get born again doesn't mean that we automatically know how to live the victorious Christian life. First, we need to learn God's ways, so we can live like God. As God's will is reflected in us and through us, then we'll appropriate His promises in our life and see total life transformation.

# Relating to God by Faith

We live in a physical, natural world. Most of us have been raised to live by our five senses: sight, hearing, smell, taste, and touch. Your inner self, or your spirit, is another sense that most people are less familiar with. You're living by your spirit when you're using your faith. In order to relate to God by the spirit, you must use your sixth sense of faith.

For example, I can't see God with my eyes, but I know He's real because I can feel Him in my heart. Likewise, if I'm experiencing sickness or pain in my body, that may be a current reality that I am experiencing in the natural world, but the Bible says that I was healed by the stripes of Jesus (1 Pet. 2:24). Or I may experience memory loss in my mind in the natural world, but the Bible says that I have the mind of Christ (1 Cor. 2:16), that I'm anointed by God, and I have all knowledge (1 John 2:20). I am using my faith when I choose to live by the truth of what God's Word says about me, instead of giving in to temporary symptoms in my soul and body.

Our experiences in the soulish realm or body, doesn't mean that it trumps the Word of God. The Word of God is truth (John 17:17), and that truth will remain for all eternity (Ps. 119:89). God's truth trumps anything that we experience in the natural realm, and it has the power to change our circumstances. The more that you continue in God's truth and live your life by it, the more you'll experience true freedom in this life (John 8:31-32). What you're seeing, feeling, or experiencing in the natural world is going to pass away; it's temporary, but the unseen realm is what you fix your eyes and hope upon because it's eternal (2 Cor. 4:18). All of life, and the earth as we know it, will pass away, including your body (1 Cor. 15:52-53), but God's Word is the incorruptible seed by which you have become born again and through which all creation was created. The Word of God will never perish (1 Pet. 1:23-25) and this is what you should base your life upon.

It takes faith to believe in things that you can't see or feel. It takes faith for me to resist pain and sickness in my body, and to trust God's Word. It takes faith to believe that you've become identical to Jesus Christ in your spirit right now in this lifetime (1 John 4:17). But this is how the believer relates to God and has fellowship with God, since God is a Spirit (John 4:24). Without the use of faith, it's impossible to please God (Heb. 11:6). But God makes it clear that His Word is Spirit and life, and it will profit your life tremendously (John 6:63). You cannot rely on the way you feel, on your actions, or on what you see in order to have a relationship with God. If you do this, then you will be unstable in your relationship with God, and it will only cause more confusion and disorder in your life. The more you relate to God by faith and the truth in the spirit, the more you'll see freedom and transformation in your life. Where the Spirit of the Lord is, there is freedom (2 Cor. 3:18). Your faith will always be needed to relate to God, and to live in the power of your new identity. As you do so, you will experience this life-transforming freedom simply by believing the truth in your heart and living your life by it—no matter what your senses are telling you.

> **Your faith will always be needed to relate to God, and to walk in your new identity.**

## A Prosperous, More Abundant Life

Jesus paid for you to have a blessed, prosperous life when He died on the cross, and He's given you the tools you need to experience it on earth! In John 10:10 NKJV, Jesus said, "The thief does not come except to steal, and to kill, and to destroy. I have come that they may have life, and that they may have it more abundantly." ⁵*More abundantly* in Greek means superabundant (in quantity), superior (in quality), excessive, exceeding abundantly above, more abundantly, beyond measure, over and above, more than is necessary, supremely. What a phenomenal promise that Jesus offers you! A life that is more than enough in every way possible.

Psalm 35:27 NKJV says, "...Let the LORD be magnified, who has pleasure in the prosperity of His servant." God delights when His children prosper. Godly prosperity is not only talking about financial prosperity, although it is included. God's type of prosperity covers every area of your life. It starts in your spirit and overflows into every area of your life. It includes your soul, body, health, finances, relationships, and every area of your life. ⁶The word *prosperity* in this verse is the Hebrew word, shalom. Most people know this word to mean *peace.* However, it means much more than that. Shalom means completeness, soundness, soundness in body, safety, welfare, health, prosperity, peace, quiet, contentment, all is well, wholly. This is God's will for you; to live a life of strength, wholeness, wellness, lacking no good thing, and to live in His shalom peace and prosperity in every area of your life.

Praise God that Jesus made a way for you to live a more abundant life through the power of His Spirit inside of you—your new identity in Christ.

## Living in Your New Identity

As you learn to live from the truths in your born again spirit, the life giving power of God will be reflected in your soul and body, producing positive results in your life. These positive results are the promises in God's Word. God promises that when we live according to the truths in His Word, our lives will be blessed, and we will walk in divine health, deliverance, prosperity, and freedom. This way of living does not require a sinless life, a strict diet, a rigid exercise program, or restrictive living. It all comes from a personal relationship with God.

---

**Godly prosperity is not only talking about financial prosperity, though it is included. God's type of prosperity covers every area of your life.**

---

From your relationship with God, the Holy Spirit and the Word will help you, give you wisdom, and reveal the truths you need to know, so you can live from who you are in the spirit. To discover who you are in the spirit, you must look to the Word of God. God's Word is a mirror (James 1:22-25), or a reflection of who you are in Christ, and that is where you will discover who you are.

## A Living Sacrifice

Since Jesus paid for all of these amazing promises, then how do you appropriate them in your life? Let's look to the Word for the answer. Romans 12:1 says, "And so, dear brothers and sisters, I plead with you to give your bodies to God because of all he has done for you. Let them be a living and holy sacrifice—the kind he will find acceptable. This is truly the way to worship him."

When you submit your will to God's will, you present your entire life to Him as a living sacrifice.

Becoming a living sacrifice means that you stop living for self and start living for God. This enables God to lead you to His promises and transform your life.

# A Transformed Life

Once you surrender your entire life to God, then He is able to lead you into victory in every area of your life. Romans 12:2 then says, "Don't copy the behavior and customs of this world, **but let God transform you into a new person** by changing the way you think. Then you will learn to know God's will for you, which is good and pleasing and perfect." When you pattern your life after the world, then your life becomes fashioned to the world and not after God. The Bible says that anyone who is a friend of the world is the enemy of God (James 4:4). God didn't send Jesus to let you live a powerless, normal, defeated life like the rest of the world. Instead, you should be *transformed into the image of God!* [7]The word *transformed* is the Greek word metamorphoo, [8]which is where the English word metamorphosis comes from. [9]The definition of this word is a change of the form or nature of a thing or person into a completely different one, by natural or supernatural means.

The same way a creepy, crawly caterpillar transforms into a beautiful, soaring butterfly, is the same way you and I can transform from an ungodly, powerless person into a supernatural, powerful child of God! You can *transform* your life to reflect an *entirely new nature* simply by surrendering your life to God, by no longer living for yourself or the way the world lives, and by renewing the way you think.

## Renewing Your Mind

> **You can transform your life to reflect an entirely new nature simply by renewing your mind to the Word of God.**

Renewing our mind and thinking differently than we used to is essential in living a transformed life. I don't know about you, but in my life, I can recognize a lot of thoughts and thought patterns that don't align with God's ways. Thankfully, God gives us tools to live our natural life with supernatural results! Let's look at Romans 12:2 again. The NKJV says, "And do not be conformed to this world, but be transformed **by the renewing of your mind,** that you may prove what is that good and acceptable and perfect will of God." [10]The word *renewing* in Greek means renovation, complete change for the better.

Have you ever renovated something? Several years ago, I picked up a side job helping a friend flip houses. He would buy foreclosed houses, fix them up, and re-sell them at a higher cost. Let me tell you about the process. Usually, these homes were rejected by the owners in many ways. The outside was stained, pieces of the siding and patios were missing, and there was overgrown grass and weeds all around the house. It was a sore sight.

Looking back, walking inside was an entirely worse experience. Layers of smells throughout the carpets and flooring needed to be pulled up and removed from the home. Before you could even start cleaning the house in order to renovate it, you had to remove the excess trash and furniture. There were dumpsters and dumpsters of trash and furniture that needed to be removed. To make it livable, you have to tear down the old, and replace it with new. These homes were usually abandoned by the owners, and it seemed like they had to leave in a hurry.

I don't know about you, but I can relate! There have been many areas of my life that needed the restoring, renovating power of God. Perhaps there is an area of your life that feels abandoned. If so, be encouraged! Any neglected area in your life can be renewed with the truth of the Word of God.

After I surrendered my life to God, I started my day with ten minutes of reading the Bible. I didn't know the power of that small habit back then, but today I see how

God used that time to begin renewing my mind! Spending time in the Word helped me to understand my new identity, and it helped me to hear God leading me. Reading the Word strengthened the voice of my conscience, which had been hardened after years and years of rejecting that quiet, powerful voice. This simple habit transformed me from the inside out and helped me to go further in my walk with God, so I could begin to pursue my purpose. Without this small habit, I would have been unable to go any further in my walk with God, let alone accomplish the amazing opportunities He's placed in my life. If you want God to transform your life like He has mine, then I encourage you to have a consistent, daily habit of reading the Word.

## Proving God's Will

The more you renovate your life and become like God, the more He can use your life for His purposes, and your life will shine with the brilliant promises of God. Let's look at Romans 12:2 again. The NKJV says, "And do not be conformed to this world, but be transformed by the renewing of your mind, **that you may prove what is that good and acceptable and perfect will of God.**"

Proving God's will in your life is progressive and it takes time. Your life will prove first the good, next the acceptable, and then the perfect will of God.

I believe this is so because it takes time to learn how to apply God's Word to our life, to fully surrender to Him, to renew our thinking, and to gain experience putting all these things together. For me, I wanted to see *all* the promises of God in my life, and I wanted to see them happen *overnight.* But God says to let patience have her perfect work in your life, so that you may be perfect and entire, lacking nothing (James 1:4). The Bible also says that faith and patience inherit the promises (Heb. 6:12). If we put these things together, then it requires time and experience, faithfully using the Word of God in our lives over the course of our lifespan, in order to see more and more of the promises come to pass.

This is so encouraging to me! No one has walked out this process perfectly, especially me. In fact, I think I made every mistake possible when I started applying God's Word to my life.

Proving God's will is a process. It takes time to understand God's Word and know how to apply it to your life with understanding. But keep reading because that's what my book is all about!

As you continue to live in your new identity, the truth in God's Word will emerge from your spirit and overflow into your physical life. This process will produce the promises of God increasingly over time, proving God's will in your everyday life.

# You Are a New Creature in Christ

For a while, I had a difficult time living in my new identity. I could see seven years of destruction in my life, relationships, and finances. I could feel seven years of emotional and physical abuse in my memories, emotions, and body. It was all so real, and *I allowed my emotions, tiredness, and pain to lead my life and my decisions.* It took time and renewing my mind to the truth for me to realize that my soul and my body were there to serve me, not to lead me. The things I could see and feel may have been a reality, but they were not the truth, and they were no longer the deciding factor.

It was hard to surrender my will, stop living by emotional whims and desires, and start listening to others. I would like to tell you how brave I was, and that I faced it all head-on with integrity, grit, and boldness. But in reality, it took everything within me to not run back to that old lifestyle. As miserable and painful as it was, that old lifestyle was all that I knew, and it was comfortable.

Sometimes, change can be the most difficult thing we face, unless we face it with Christ. Once I truly understood that I was not the sum of my past, and that the real me was righteous, holy, strong, and redeemed in Christ, then it became easier for me to stop focusing on what I could see, and start living by who I was in Christ. Something that really helped me with this was a mentor.

It was suggested to me early in my recovery to get a mentor—someone wiser than me that I could call every day—to seek advice, wisdom, and guidance. This meant that if I was truly surrendered, then I could call this person, tell them what was going on, and if they gave me direction, then I would submit to their instruction. I had tried this many times over the past seven years, but it never produced the results it should have because I wasn't truly surrendered. This time, however, was different. I was so tired of producing poor results in my life that I was desperate to see something change and obey other people's orders. Finally, I was a surrendered, living sacrifice. This meant that if I wanted to do something that didn't align with God's Word or my mentor's instruction, then I didn't do it. This became a daily, sometimes every minute, practice of laying down my will, so that I could allow God's will to be done in my life. Even though I didn't do this perfectly, it was still getting ingrained and trained within me *as my new norm*. Finally, God was in His rightful place in my life, and He was able to help me and lead me.

This worked so much for me, and produced such amazing results, that I still have a mentor today. Sometimes, my emotions and my will can be so powerful that it can be difficult for me to think straight. Instead of relying on what I think or what I want, I can call this person when I don't know what to do, or when I need guidance and support. This helps me to keep my will pure and aligned with God. I try to follow this principle in everything I do, even though I don't do it perfectly. Whether I'm relying on my mentors, or relying on God's Word for guidance, I always think it's helpful to have wise counsel—someone wiser than me who I can trust, be honest with, and glean from their wisdom and experience.

Through that experience, I can see that *God taught me how to listen to someone else, so that eventually, I could listen to and obey His quiet voice within me.* His leadership each and every day is the *ultimate* wise Counsellor that we should rely upon minute by minute.

This picture of mentorship is a great example for how to work out what the Word is telling us in Romans 12:1-

2. Become a living sacrifice, don't conform to the world, and renew the way we think. If we do these things, we are truly submitted to God, and we will see transformation in our life through the good, acceptable, and perfect will of God.

> Therefore if anyone is in Christ [that is, grafted in, joined to Him by faith in Him as Savior], he is a new creature [reborn and renewed by the Holy Spirit]; the old things [the previous moral and spiritual condition] have passed away. Behold, new things have come [because spiritual awakening brings a new life]. (2 Corinthians 5:17 AMP)

---

**From this place, you are better equipped to live the Christian life filled with supernatural power from the Holy Spirit, which equips you to fulfill your God-given destiny.**

---

Your old life is gone, and a new life has emerged! Now, you can live by the truths in God's Word, instead of listening to the way you feel in your mind, will, emotions, and body. When you do this, you are living by faith in your new identity in Christ. From this place, you are better equipped to live the Christian life filled with supernatural power from the Holy Spirit, which equips you to fulfill your God-given destiny.

Understanding who you are in Christ will help you to walk in your new identity. Instead of focusing on who you were in the past, or even decisions you may have made today, you can focus on who you are in your spirit.

These truths, and renewing your mind to these truths, will help you to live a transformed life. This life of transformation is the life that God intended you to live all along. He intended for you to live in health, happiness, prosperity, and deliverance all the days of your life.

If you believe that this is true, and you want to apply it to your life immediately, then here is a personal declaration to speak out of your mouth:

*My new identity in Christ has empowered me to unlock the fullness of my potential. My life is being transformed as I become a living sacrifice and renew my mind with the truth. I live my life from my new identity, and I am equipped with God's ability!*

# Transform Your Life
## Application of Chapter Concepts

### A Moment of Reflection: A New Life in Christ

1. Evaluate your thoughts and your current circumstances (spirit, soul, body, health, finances, relationships).
   - In what areas are you experiencing less than "life more abundantly?" How would you like to see those areas transformed by the power of Christ?
   - For example: I would like to see healing in my body and live a healthy lifestyle. I would like to be debt free, and financially secure. I would like to have good relationships. I would like to be free from depression.
   - Ask God to help you restore these areas of your life through His love and the truth in His Word.

2. What is He speaking to you about these areas, and revealing to you about your future?

- Spend time alone with God, and let Him guide your heart.

3. What is He leading you to do next? Listen to His voice, and write down thoughts that come to your mind. Remember, God's voice will always agree with the Word. If a thought comes that contradicts God's Word, you can replace it with the truth.

## My Transformation Scripture

What is a scripture that speaks to you about who you are in Christ? Here are a few suggestions:
- My old self has been crucified with Christ. It is no longer I who live, but Christ lives in me. So I live in this earthly body by trusting in the Son of God, who loved me and gave himself for me. (Galatians 2:20)
- And as we live in God, our love grows more perfect. So we will not be afraid on the day of judgment, but we can face him with confidence because we live like Jesus here in this world. (1 John 4:17)
- A final word: Be strong in the Lord and in his mighty power. (Ephesians 6:10)

- Each time he said, "My grace is all you need. My power works best in weakness." So now I am glad to boast about my weaknesses, so that the power of Christ can work through me. (2 Corinthians 12:9)
- For I can do everything through Christ, who gives me strength. (Philippians 4:13)
- This means that anyone who belongs to Christ has become a new person. The old life is gone; a new life has begun! (2 Corinthians 5:17)
- And because we are his children, God has sent the Spirit of his Son into our hearts, prompting us to call out, "Abba, Father." (Galatians 4:6)
- Don't you realize that all of you together are the temple of God and that the Spirit of God lives in you? (1 Corinthians 3:16)
- For we live by believing and not by seeing. (2 Corinthians 5:7)

Write the scripture that you chose in your journal. Meditate on this verse throughout the day, and remind yourself of God's perfect plan for your life.

## Time in His Presence

Spend some time with God meditating on this scripture. What do you think the Lord is speaking to you through this verse?

## Life Application

Ask the Holy Spirit to help you apply this scripture to your daily life. How can you apply this to your life today?

## Prayer

If you recognize that Christ lives in you and that He has provided you with a new life, then please pray with me:

*Lord, thank You for sending Your Son to this world, so I can live in an intimate relationship with You. I open my mind and heart to You. Help me to do Your will by Your strength so I can fulfill Your purpose for my life. Help me to walk in the promises and acknowledge every good thing in me in Christ, in Jesus' name. Amen.*

# Chapter 3

# Born Again Power

### Living Life by the Power of Heaven

*But you will receive power when the Holy Spirit comes upon you...*
—Acts 1:8

When I surrendered to God, I decided that I didn't know what was best for my life anymore. I stopped living life for myself and I stopped being the god of my life. I yielded my life and my decisions to God, which allowed the

Holy Spirit to help me and direct my life. Slowly, my mind was being renewed from my new, healthy habit of reading the Bible every day. My thoughts began to change. With my mind and heart aligning with God's mind and heart, I was able to make better decisions—godly decisions. I could discern good from evil, and I listened to the voice of my moral compass (the Holy Spirit) within me more readily. It became easier for me to live according to godliness instead of living like the world—which I was so familiar with. As I did this, day after day after day, my life became *transformed by the Word and Spirit of God within me.* The Spirit of God worked with me, helping me to be usable for the purposes of making His Kingdom known here on earth.

No one is perfect (except for Jesus). We have all sinned and lived short of the goodness and glory of God (Rom. 3:23). But we don't have to stay there. God has promised us an abundant life on earth, if we live according to the principles He has set forth in His Word. *To walk in the promises of God is to renew our mind to the Word of God and let the Holy Spirit guide us every step of the way.* Praise God that we don't accomplish this through our own works, strength, or ability—we can only accomplish this by His grace through our faith.

But—When God our Savior revealed his kindness and love, he saved us, not because of the righteous things we had done, but because of his mercy. He washed away our sins, giving us a new birth and new life through the Holy Spirit. He generously poured out the Spirit upon us through Jesus Christ our Savior. Because of his grace he made us right in his sight and gave us confidence that we will inherit eternal life. This is a trustworthy saying, and I want you to insist on these teachings so that all who trust in God will devote themselves to doing good. These teachings are good and beneficial for everyone. (Titus 3:4-8)

The love of God has appeared to all mankind, and we can experience the fruit of this love in different ways. Just as a man and his wife must continue to express their love to one another after they say, "I do," so must you and I continue to pursue God after you say, "I believe." There is more of God's power and ability to work on your behalf that you can experience on this earth. The more that you renew your mind to His ways, the more you will prove His promises through the power of the Holy Spirit working in you, and you will walk in His perfect will for your life. The

Holy Spirit is the power of God in you to accomplish the impossible for you.

## The Baptism of the Holy Spirit

When you receive Christ as your Lord and Savior, you receive the Holy Spirit inside of you. This is called the new birth, and you become born again. Before this time, your spirit was dead because of sin, and you were separated from God. Through your faith in Jesus, you become alive, forgiven for a lifetime of sin, and you are united with God. Your old nature has passed away, and now, by the Spirit of God in you, you have received Christ's nature in your spirit man. After you receive Jesus as your Lord, the next step is to receive the baptism of the Holy Spirit. The baptism of the Holy Spirit is the power of God within you. He gives you a new life, a new heart, and He quickens your mortal body. His Spirit within you will lead you and guide you into all truth. This is how God fills you with His power, His ability, and His anointing in your life. This is how you live the victorious Christian life. If you haven't received the baptism of the Holy Spirit, turn to Appendix B, where I explain it in more detail. This is an essential next step, so make sure you've received this crucial part of your faith!

Romans 8:11 says, "The Spirit of God, who raised Jesus from the dead, lives in you. And just as God raised Christ Jesus from the dead, he will give life to your mortal bodies by this same Spirit living within you." The Holy Spirit is the life source of Jesus Christ and He is your life source, too. He quickens your soul and body with resurrection power to live the Christian life.

John the Baptist came to the earth to prepare people to receive Jesus Christ, our Messiah. He educated people and told them what to look forward to.

> I baptize with water those who repent of their sins and turn to God. But someone is coming soon who is greater than I am—so much greater that I'm not worthy even to be his slave and carry his sandals. **He will baptize you with the Holy Spirit and with fire.** (Matthew 3:11)

John told us to look forward to Christ's coming because He would baptize us with the Holy Spirit—something that no man can do apart from Christ.

I lived several years of my life without the baptism of the Holy Spirit. I had never heard of Him even though I grew up in church. As soon as I found out that there was more of God for me to receive, I ran to receive the baptism of the Holy Spirit. Finally, my life was filled with the power of God that I needed. My life was filled with His presence, and a personal relationship. Bondages were broken from my life, and I became free. Not only that, but I was able to understand the Word of God in a new way, and the Holy Spirit taught me how to apply the Word to my life. He is your Teacher, Comforter, Helper, and Friend. If there is more of God to receive, why wouldn't you want to go deeper with Him! I've lived life both ways, and life with the Holy Spirit is the better way.

> **As soon as I found out that there was more of God for me to receive, I ran to receive the baptism of the Holy Spirit. Finally, my life was filled with the power of God that I needed.**

## Power from Heaven

Before Jesus left the earth, He told His disciples that He would not leave them alone; that He would send a Helper.

John 14:16-18 says,

And I will ask the Father, and he will give you another Advocate, who will never leave you. He is the Holy Spirit, who leads into all truth. The world cannot receive him, because it isn't looking for him and doesn't recognize him. But you know him, because he lives with you now and later will be in you. No, I will not abandon you as orphans—I will come to you.

Then, Jesus told the disciples twice to wait for the Holy Spirit because they would receive power from heaven.

> **...Do not leave Jerusalem until the Father sends you the gift he promised**, as I told you before. John baptized with water, but in just a few days you will be baptized with the Holy Spirit. **But you will receive power when the Holy Spirit comes upon you.** And you will be my witnesses, telling people about me everywhere—in Jerusalem, throughout Judea, in Samaria, and to the ends of the earth. (Acts 1:4-5, 8)

And now I will send the Holy Spirit, just as my Father promised. **But stay here in the city until the Holy Spirit comes and fills you with power from heaven.** (Luke 24:49)

Jesus was talking to people who had already believed in Him, yet He told them to wait, that there was more power to receive! After you receive the baptism of the Holy Spirit, it is His job to fill your life with the power of God, help you, comfort you, and lead you into all truth (John 16:13).

> **After you receive the baptism of the Holy Spirit, it is His job to fill your life with the power of God, help you, comfort you, and lead you into all truth.**

After I rededicated my life to God, I spent time in the Word, but it was hard for me to understand it and apply it to my life. Also, I continued to view myself as a drug addict, a failure, and like my life was going to amount to nothing. Three years after I got sober, I learned about the baptism of the Holy Spirit, and received Him with open arms and an open heart. I have never been the same. I was able to throw off old identities and mindsets that were holding me captive, and I was finally able to walk in the newness of life that God's Word promises. My life was becoming transformed by the power of God. I began to walk in intimacy with God, and the Holy Spirit taught me how to apply the Word of God to my life. I learned how to talk to God, how to discern when God was leading me, and He taught me as a loving Father would teach a child.

## Strengthened with Might in Your Inner Man

In Paul's letter to the Ephesian church, he prays for them. Ephesians 3:16-20 says,

> I pray that from his glorious, unlimited resources he will empower you with inner strength through his Spirit. Then Christ will make his home in your hearts as you trust in him. Your roots will grow down into God's love and keep you strong. And may you have the power to understand, as all God's people should, how wide, how long, how high, and how deep his love is. May you experience the love of Christ, though it is too great to understand fully. Then you will be made complete with all the fullness of life and power

that comes from God. Now all glory to God, who is able, through his mighty power at work within us, to accomplish infinitely more than we might ask or think.

There are many things that you can glean from this prayer. First of all, he says, "I pray that from his glorious, unlimited resources he will empower you with inner strength through his Spirit." This reveals to me that it's not automatic. If Paul is praying for these things, then it hasn't already happened, and it's not based on just being born again. However, it is according to God's riches of glory—not yours. You don't have to *produce* anything because God already has. However, *you can tap into this power when you are strengthened with might by His Spirit in your inner man. The Holy Spirit in you strengthens you with might!* In verse 17 he says, "Then Christ will make his home in your hearts as you trust in him." *The longer you walk with God, trusting Him and living by His truth, the more natural these things become to you. This causes the spiritual roots in your heart to grow into God's love and keep you strong along your journey of life.*

Then verses 18 and 19 say, "And may you have the power to understand, as all God's people should, how wide, how long, how high, and how deep his love is. May you experience the love of Christ, though it is too great to understand fully. Then you will be made complete with all the fullness of life and power that comes from God." These verses tell you that *the more you grow in experiential knowledge of the depths of God's love for you, the more you will be made complete, or whole in your spirit, soul, and body, and filled with the fullness of life and power of God.* Can you imagine what that would look like in your life, to be complete, whole, and filled with the fullness of God's life and power? It fills me with awe, wonder, and amazement just trying to imagine it. And it causes me to realize that there is so much more of God for me to experience! This also tells me that the fruit of God's promises comes from the inside out, not the outside in. You and I have a part to play in receiving God's awesome promises.

He concludes in verse 20, "Now all glory to God, who is able, through his mighty power at work within us, to accomplish infinitely more than we might ask or think." *God's power within you is able to accomplish extremely, enormously, eternally more than you could even dream, think, or ask for! But it is all according to His mighty power that works in you.* [1]The word *power* in this verse is translated in Greek to mean force, capacity, competency, freedom, mastery, superhuman, token of control, delegated influence, authority, liberty, power, right, and strength.

Do you need some of God's divine strength, ability, and power in your life? I sure do! The baptism of the Holy Spirit is the power of God working in you and through you to initiate growth, freedom, and transformation in your life. Without it, you are missing the power of God that you need to live the victorious Christian life. His power becomes your power. God's power fills you with ability, capacity, freedom, and strength—the ability of God to take control of every area of your life! This is the power that the church needs to walk in the fullness of God and take the gospel to the ends of the world. In order to apply God's Word to your life and walk in the power of God, you need the baptism of the Holy Spirit.

---

**The baptism of the Holy Spirit is the power of God working in you and through you to initiate growth, freedom, and transformation in your life.**

# You Can Do All Things through a Supernatural Turn-around

After getting clean from drugs, I slowly began to apply spiritual principles to my life that I was learning from the Bible. I began to seek God with my whole heart, but it wasn't always easy. I was learning how to trust God, and resist lies, temptation, and the ungodly desires within me. I was learning how to lean on the wisdom of my loving Father, even though my emotions were telling me otherwise. People would encourage me and say, "God has His hand on you. You are going to help so many people one day." I would smile in disbelief and think to myself, *don't they know what I've done?* Inside, it hurt so bad at times. I struggled to believe that God could truly redeem my life and all the decisions I had made. I thought I ruined my life for good. I was in debt, filed bankruptcy, no professional resume, and I had the emotional maturity of a 14-year-old in a 23-year-old's body. I didn't know how to be an adult, let alone manage my own life. One step at a time, decision after decision, I surrendered my will and chose God's will.

One of the best decisions I made was spending time with God each day. I would start by praising and thanking Him for loving me and being so good to me. I would pray, listen, and just be quiet. I would read the Word and try to apply it to my life as He led me. This habit became an integral part of my relationship with God, and it's the most important, fulfilling, and fun part of my day. This time with God gives Him an opportunity to lead me and direct my heart.

Early in my sobriety, before I received the baptism of the Holy Spirit, I felt like God was asking me to quit smoking cigarettes. I tried and failed many times, so I switched to smoking an e-cig, and moved on with my life. After a couple years, I realized that I had not heard God leading me. When I asked Him why, He said, "I'm still waiting for you to do what I told you to do." Wow! God was not going to give me my next step until I accomplished what He told me to do first.

So, I tried to quit smoking again. It was hard, and I was struggling. Finally, I cried out to God, and said, "God! If this doesn't get easier, I'm going back to smoking!" The next day I woke up and every desire to smoke was gone. All He was waiting for, was for me to ask Him for help. Every time I try to do something in my own ability, I fail. But when I rely on God for everything, He is there, like a loving Father, ready to show Himself strong on my behalf.

Each time he said, "My grace is all you need. My power works best in weakness." So now I am glad to boast about my weaknesses, so that the power of Christ can work through me. (2 Corinthians 12:9)

I understand that not everyone is familiar with the baptism of the Holy Spirit, and some people are weary of it because of prior experience or religion. As you can see, God was still able to lead me before I had the baptism of the Holy Spirit, but it was so difficult for me to do things God was asking me to do. It was even difficult for me to understand my new identity and how to apply these spiritual principles in my natural life. It's not a deal-breaker if you don't receive the baptism of the Holy Spirit—you will still go to heaven just by being born again. However, it will truly limit God's ability working in you. Your life will not have the power, strength, and ability of God to live a supernatural life. Today, I look back and see complete restoration and redemption in every area of my life, and it all happened as a result of the baptism of the Holy Spirit. In fact, the places that were ruined and full of ashes are now sparkling with hope and purpose. I don't believe that would have been possible without the baptism of the Holy Spirit. I do things today that make me shake and tremble, but I know it's not me who's doing it, it's the Holy Spirit within me, helping my inability and comforting me in my faith.

> I pray that God, the source of hope, will fill you completely with joy and peace because you trust in him. Then you will overflow with confident hope **through the power of the Holy Spirit.** (Romans 15:13)

The Holy Spirit is your gift from the Father to equip you and anoint you with His ability in you. You no longer have to rely on yourself and know the right thing to do every step of the way. The Holy Spirit will lead you with the Word and peace of God to show you the next step. With this divine power from heaven, God can lead your life to complete restoration and victory. As the Holy Spirit leads you to the will of God, He will equip you with strength to walk in God's will in every area of your life. Power from heaven will propel you to fulfill your God-given purpose on the earth. You can do all things through the power of Christ within you. This empowered lifestyle will lead you to the life that God intended you to live with Him.

# Transform Your Life

## Application of Chapter Concepts

### A Moment of Reflection: A Life of Power

1. Think back through your life. Has there been a time when you felt powerless and alone?

    - The Holy Spirit is Christ in you, and He never leaves you or forsakes you. You are never alone, even when you feel alone. Ask Him to reveal His truth to you about that time in your life.

2. The Holy Spirit will never force His will in your life. In what area(s) are you inviting Him to lead you?

3. How would you like the power of the Holy Spirit to redeem and restore certain areas of your life? What would it look like to live a life influenced by God's power? Be specific as you highlight His promises in every area of your life:

- In your spirit:
- In your soul:
- In your body:
- In your health:
- In your finances:
- In your relationships:
- In your career:

4. Spend time alone with God, and let Him guide your heart. What is He leading you to do next? Listen to His voice, and write down thoughts that come to your mind.

## My Transformation Scripture

What is a scripture that speaks to you about the Holy Spirit? Here are a few suggestions:

- I pray that God, the source of hope, will fill you completely with joy and peace because you trust in him. Then you will overflow with confident hope through the power of the Holy Spirit. (Romans 15:13)
- But you will receive power when the Holy Spirit comes upon you. And you will be my witnesses, telling people about me everywhere—in Jerusalem,

throughout Judea, in Samaria, and to the ends of the earth. (Acts 1:8)

- For all who are led by the Spirit of God are children of God. So you have not received a spirit that makes you fearful slaves. Instead, you received God's Spirit when he adopted you as his own children. Now we call him, "Abba, Father." (Romans 8:14-15)
- And I will pray the Father, and He will give you another Helper, that He may abide with you forever. (John 14:16 NKJV)
- However, when He, the Spirit of truth, has come, He will guide you into all truth; for He will not speak on His own authority, but whatever He hears He will speak; and He will tell you things to come. (John 16:13 NKJV)
- But the Holy Spirit produces this kind of fruit in our lives: love, joy, peace, patience, kindness, goodness, faithfulness, gentleness, and self-control. There is no law against these things! (Galatians 5:22-23)

## Time in His Presence

Write the scripture that you chose in your journal. Meditate on this verse throughout the day, and remind yourself of God's perfect plan for your life.

## Life Application

Ask Holy Spirit to help you apply this scripture to your daily life. How can you apply this to your life today?

## Prayer

If you acknowledge that the Holy Spirit lives in you and that He has power and purpose for your life, then please pray with me:

*Lord, thank You for sending Your Holy Spirit to live inside of me to guide me into Your truth and have intimacy with You. I receive everything that You have for me because I know that it's good. Holy Spirit, I invite You into every area of my life. Fill my life with Your presence and power, so I can fulfill Your purpose for my life. In Jesus' name. Amen.*

# Chapter 4

## The Power of the Word

### Releasing God's Will in Your Life

*For the word of God is alive and powerful. It is sharper than the sharpest two-edged sword, cutting between soul and spirit, between joint and marrow. It exposes our innermost thoughts and desires.*
—Hebrews 4:12

Understanding God's love for me, along with my new identity in Christ, set me on a firm foundation in my walk with God. The baptism of the Holy Spirit filled me with supernatural power and ability that lifted me from an old, hopeless identity to a *new life* full of passion, power, and purpose. Hope was finally within reach, and I was ready to tackle the world by faith! But wait. I realized that the Word is full of promises that I had yet to see come to pass in my life. I asked myself, *What's the point of being a Christian if my life hasn't been changed?* I was starting to *feel* a difference on the inside, which gave me hope, but I sincerely wanted to *see* a change on the outside. I wanted to see the healing, prosperity, deliverance, and the freedom that God's Word promised me. Maybe I had more grit inside of me than I thought I did, because giving up just wasn't in my DNA. Pressing forward was the only option, and I had tasted enough of God's goodness to know that I was headed in the right direction.

Here's a sneak peek for you that I wish I would've known back then: God's Word must be planted in your heart like a seed to see its fruit in your everyday life. As you learn how to follow the direction that the Word gives you, and sow this seed into your heart, it will automatically produce fruit and freedom in every area of your life.

This is the understanding I needed to start *seeing* natural evidence of my Christian faith. This is why God tells us to be patient in our faith, because in due season, we will reap a harvest (Gal. 6:9).

# The Word is Full of Power

God's Word is alive, powerful, and inspired by God Himself. In fact, the Holy Spirit helped each person who wrote the Word of God as we know it. Holy men of God wrote the Word of God as they were moved, or inspired, by the Spirit of God in them. God did this so that through His Word we would have His divine wisdom and leadership for our lives. The Bible is God's manual to mankind. It is His love letter, His instruction, His divine hand, and guidance in our life to show us the proper paths to take while we are on this earth. The Bible guides our lives into godliness as individuals, and beyond that, it aids us as we build our families, government systems, schools, businesses, and every sphere of life that you can imagine.

> All Scripture is inspired by God and is useful to teach us what is true and to make us realize what is wrong in our lives. It corrects us when we are wrong and teaches us to do what is right. God uses it to prepare and equip his people to do every good work.
> (2 Timothy 3:16-17)

This verse tells us that all scripture is inspired by God and that all scripture is useful to us. Knowing what God's Word says is helpful! We can use His Word to discover what is the absolute truth, correct what is wrong in our lives, and to prepare us for His purpose.

God's Word can also speak to you, heal you, help you, and instruct you. The Word of God is alive, powerful, and able to aid every area of your life!

> For the word of God is alive and powerful. It is sharper than the sharpest two-edged sword, cutting between soul and spirit, between joint and marrow. It exposes our innermost thoughts and desires. (Hebrews 4:12)

The Word of God has supernatural power within it that can restore your soul and heal your body. It is where you discover the truth about God, gain spiritual knowledge, wisdom, and understanding, and grow in discernment. Another way of saying this is that it helps you mature spiritually. Spending time with the Word of God is like washing your soul with purifying water, cleansing you from the inside out. It can speak to your heart, and direct you in the way of peace. God's Word is full of wisdom and power for the believer!

# God Speaks Through the Word

Jesus says, in John 10:27, "My sheep listen to my voice; I know them, and they follow me." When you are saved, you receive the ability to hear God's voice through the Spirit of Christ within you.

Early in my Christian walk, I didn't know that I could have an intimate relationship with God, and I didn't know that I could hear His voice. I didn't know that He had a specific plan for my life, nor did I know that He loved me deeply. After I learned these things, not only did I begin to practice applying them to my life, but I also began to practice hearing God's voice. Along the way, I discovered that most people don't hear the audible voice of God. Rather, God's voice sounds like your own voice. It sounds like your own thoughts; an inner knowing, a witness within your heart, or even peace. God can speak to us in many ways: through your conscience, through the Word, through the Spirit of God within you, and through the Holy Spirit and gifts of the Spirit (1 Cor. 12).

When you seek God through the renewing of your mind and living according to God's Word, it will come alive within you. The Word will speak to you and guide you. God will use the Word to direct your life into His fullness. God's

Word is a lamp to your feet and a light to your path (Ps. 119:105). This is why it's so important to know God's Word, so that when you hear God's voice, you can say, "yes, that aligns with God's Word and will."

When you hear the truth, the Spirit of God bear's witness with your heart, and you will recognize the truth, so you can follow it.

## You Have a New Mirror

When you look into your mirror at home, what do you see? You may see your reflection and take it at face value. But if you are like me and so many others, you may also see your past, or you may be able to see the way you feel that day. Some people might see the imperfections about themselves that they dislike so much. Or maybe a lifetime of regret is hidden behind the expressions on their face. Even if you can see all of these things in your mirror at home, there are still things that you can't see. The way you feel in your soul is expressed through your thoughts and emotions, which are unseen. Your body may tell you how it feels through comfort, discomfort, pain, and so forth. All of those things are unseen with your eyes. For example, if I were to ask you right now, "How are you feeling today?" You could instantly tell me something like, "I feel happy." Perfect. Likewise, if I were to ask you, "What does your body feel like right now?" you might respond by saying, "My body feels good, but I have a little pain in my back." This is all great, and normal.

If there are basic, normal things that you experience every day that you *can't see* in your mirror at home, then why couldn't there be an *entirely additional* part of you on the inside that you have yet to experience the fullness of? There is more to you than what you can see with your eyes, feel in your emotions, think in your thoughts, and experience in your physical body. Your spirit has become brand new and identical to Jesus Christ when you get born again. This *new part of you* has far more power and potential within it that can override the things you're feeling and experiencing right now.

You have the Spirit, identity, righteousness, and holiness of Jesus Christ Himself in your spirit. All of His power, promises, presence, and perfection can be drawn out of your inner man, through your soul, and into your body. This is living life from the inside out—from the truth of who you are in Christ. Jesus told the people who already believed in Him a conditional statement. He said, "*if* you do x, y, or z, *then* you will receive this." Let's look at it together.

So Jesus was saying to those Jews who had believed Him, "**If you continue in My word,** then you are truly My disciples; **and you will know the truth, and the truth will set you free.**" (John 8:31-32 NASB)

The more truth you know that is hidden within the Word of God, and the more you continue to live by it in your daily life, the more freedom you will experience every day, in every area of your life. You and the life around you will be transformed into the new creature that you already are in the spirit. All of the promises in God's Word can come to pass through your new identity in Christ. Promises like peace, healing, provision, prosperity, joy, love, kindness, gentleness, purpose, and on and on they go. These aren't just promises that the body of Christ is striving to receive in their life, but also promises that *you can become.* You transform into a peaceful, joyful person who emanates the love and life of God everywhere you go. If there's any area of your life that's lacking the complete prosperity of God, then the mirror of God's Word is the answer.

The Word of God is your spiritual mirror (James 1:25). It is a reflection of Christ, and who you are in your spirit. As you spend more and more time in the Word, it will help you to discover who you are, and the purpose God has for you. When you look to the Word of God, you will see who you truly are, and you will be equipped to walk it out. The Bible refers to this as being a hearer and a doer of the Word.

> But don't just listen to God's word. You must do what it says. Otherwise, you are only fooling yourselves. For if you listen to the word and don't obey, it is like glancing at your face in a mirror. You see yourself, walk away, and forget what you look like. But if you look carefully into the perfect law that sets you free, and if you do what it says and don't forget what you heard, then God will bless you for doing it.
> (James 1:22-25)

I could also sum up this verse as *continuing* in the Word, like I pointed out in John 8:31-32. The Word needs to be a priority, an essential factor in the believer's life. My life wouldn't have been *transformed* if I just visited the Word at church on Sunday morning. As a daily habit, I familiarized myself with the mirror of God's Word. I discovered my new identity in Christ and relied on those truths instead of my past or even present circumstances. This equipped me to continue in the Word and become a doer of the Word. It took time for me to renew my mind to these truths, so that I could say, "This may be how I feel right now, but I know what God's Word says. I have the love, joy, peace, and kindness of God in my spirit, so I am going to act on that today." When you see who you are in the Word and then follow through with it by doing it in your life, it changes you. This is one way that your life becomes changed and transformed by God's Word, and how you begin to *see and feel* the evidence of your faith; the evidence of God's promises in the natural world.

## The Word Is a Seed

The Bible teaches us that the Word of God is a seed and that it cannot die. It is incorruptible, abiding forever.

> Having been born again, not of corruptible seed but incorruptible, through the word of God which lives and abides forever. (1 Peter 1:23 NKJV)

You are born again by the incorruptible seed of God's Word, which will remain for all eternity (Psalm 119:89). The Word of God that you know, believe, become intimate with, and plant within your heart will remain with you forever. To plant the Word in your heart, you must believe it. When you plant the seed of God's Word in the soil of your heart, it will bring forth fruit. The amount of fruit you produce from the Word depends on the soil of your heart.

> **To plant the Word in your heart, you must believe it.**

## The Soil of Your Heart

In Mark 4 and other Gospels, the farmer sowed the Word, and the soil was people's hearts. Mark 4:15-20 tells you that the soil of your heart will determine the amount of fruit that you will produce from the seed of God's Word. Let's look at these verses together from the Book of Matthew.

> The seed that fell on the footpath represents those who hear the message about the Kingdom and don't understand it. Then the evil one comes and snatches away the seed that was planted in their hearts [soil #1]. The seed on the rocky soil represents those who hear the message and immediately receive it with joy. But since they don't have deep roots, they don't

last long. They fall away as soon as they have problems or are persecuted for believing God's word [soil #2]. The seed that fell among the thorns represents those who hear God's word, but all too quickly the message is crowded out by the worries of this life and the lure of wealth, so no fruit is produced [soil #3]. The seed that fell on good soil represents those who truly hear and understand God's word and produce a harvest of thirty, sixty, or even a hundred times as much as had been planted [soil #4]! (Matthew 13:19-23 [brackets mine])

Since my husband and I have a garden at home, I find that this parable has come to life for me. The soil of our garden *definitely* matters, and it can determine the harvest of all our hard work. To help paint a better picture of these verses, I will compare each soil with my garden at home.

**Soil #1** believes in God but lacks an understanding of the Word. In our garden, there are so many predators that the plants need protection from. To ensure they will stay safe, we have built raised beds with row covers, and a fence around the beds. Soil #1 needs to protect the seeds they plant in their hearts through understanding the Word of God. Without an understanding, Satan can come and steal the Word from your heart, and it won't produce a harvest.

As an active drug addict, I remember reading this parable while I was sitting in my bed one day. I recall feeling frustrated because I didn't understand what all of this meant, but I knew that the Word wasn't changing my life. I don't know if you can relate, but if you can, God sees your hungry heart, and He is ready to give you an understanding of His Word. This is why it's so important to understand God's Word and how to apply it to your life. If you read or hear the Word and don't understand it, Satan comes immediately to steal the Word out of your heart. Receiving the baptism of the Holy Spirit helped me to understand the Word tremendously, and I found a teacher that teaches the Word of God correctly, Andrew Wommack. Andrew and his wife, Jamie, are the founders and presidents of Andrew Wommack Ministries and Charis Bible College; a global ministry that focuses on spreading the gospel of Jesus Christ to ends of the earth, while discipling believers around the world. God has used the Holy Spirit and Andrew Wommack to help me comprehend the Word and apply it to my life with wisdom and understanding.

**Soil #2** hears the Word, but they haven't had time to apply it to their life and get it rooted in their heart. With all my plants at home, I started them from seeds, so they are very fragile. Before planting them in the great Colorado outdoors, they must grow a certain amount, and they need water and special light. This will help them to be well rooted and strong outside. Early in my Christian life, I tried to immediately act on different verses within the Bible, which caused pain and tribulation in my life. Instead, I could have tried to believe the Word and wait for it to bring fruit in my life. Now that I understand this principle, it has helped me to get the Word rooted in my heart, and I am seeing much more fruit.

**Soil #3** receives the Word, but there are rocks and thorns—other things in the soil that choke the Word, and harm the harvest. When I am working in our garden, I remove limbs, weeds, or large pieces of mulch that look like they could hurt the plants. In my relationship with God today, He is continually alerting me when I am allowing cares, worries, or distractions to enter into my heart. God knows that those things damage my harvest. As a good gardener of my heart, I try to monitor that state of my heart continually, checking for stress, worry, anxiety, bitterness, and offense. If I see any of these things, then I quickly take my open heart to God, so He can help me safely remove them. This is a big reason why a daily habit of time with God is so important. This quiet time in His presence allows Him to bring things to my attention, so that we can take care of it together.

**Soil #4** is good soil. It is well protected with a good root system and free from debris. This heart has had time with God and the Word. They have taken the knowledge that they have gleaned from the Word and understood how to apply it to their life with wisdom. When situations and circumstances arise, their relationship with God is a refuge they can run to, to receive help, nourishment, safety, and assistance removing unnecessary perils from their precious heart. As a result, the Word automatically brings forth fruit, and they receive a great harvest.

The more you understand the Word, become rooted in the Word, and remove the cares and distractions of the world from your life, the more your heart will become good soil, and will bring forth more fruit from God's Word.

## A Harvest Takes Time to Grow

It takes time to bring forth any type of harvest, spiritually or naturally. Just as a farmer can't plant seeds today and receive a harvest tomorrow, neither can a believer find a scripture to believe today and expect to see it in their life tomorrow. It takes time to nurture and cultivate those seeds in order to promote the proper growth stages.

While the earth remaineth, seedtime and harvest, and cold and heat, and summer and winter, and day and night shall not cease. (Genesis 8:22 KJV)

Jesus also said, in Mark 4:26-29,

"The Kingdom of God is like a farmer who scatters seed on the ground. Night and day, while he's asleep or awake, the seed sprouts and grows, but he does not understand how it happens. The earth produces the crops on its own. First a leaf blade pushes through, then the heads of wheat are formed, and finally the grain ripens. And as soon as the grain is ready, the farmer comes and harvests it with a sickle, for the harvest time has come."

Genesis 8:22 tells you that while the earth remains, seedtime, harvest, the seasons, and day and night will remain. Mark 4:26-29 tells you that there are natural, earthly principles that help us relate to the kingdom of God. Jesus uses this example of a farmer planting a seed in the ground and taking care of the seed. The earth, or the soil of your heart, will produce the crop on its own once it's been planted in your heart. Finally, it will be a sprout, next a stalk, and then you will see the fruit, and it's ready for you to harvest. This helps me to understand that I can't bypass the spiritual or natural laws that God has set in place of which this is one of many. The Word is a seed that takes time to produce fruit in the believing heart.

> **The Word is a seed that takes time to produce fruit in the believing heart.**

Please learn from my mistakes as I candidly tell you how not to do this. I tried to force the fruit from God's Word into my life overnight. This happened time and time again by standing on the Word and expecting to see a harvest immediately. One time, I stopped taking my thyroid medication because my thyroid had been removed several years prior, and I wanted to see God's healing in my life. I stood my ground for several months and I nearly died without my medication. My body became swollen, I lost a lot of hair, and I had no energy. My organs were shutting down, my skin was orange, and I was losing control of my emotions and body movements. Finally, it dawned on me, that what I was doing wasn't godly, nor was it from God. I started taking the medication again, and immediately my body began to repair itself. I learned that bluntly using my faith to believe for one of God's promises is not the way to do it. God wasn't mad at me for trying to stand on the Word and have faith for my healing, but there is a better way to do it. The better way would have been to sow seeds of like kind in my heart, meditate on them consistently, give it some time, and be patient for my harvest.

## Sow Seeds You Want to Eat

To use our garden as a reference again, we wanted to sow multiple types of seeds so that we could eat several different fruits and vegetables throughout the season. To receive a harvest of variety, we needed to plant multiple types of seeds. If we wanted to have corn to eat, then we needed to plant corn seeds. We also wanted peppers, strawberries, cantaloupe, and spinach, so we bought those seeds, and planted them. We nourished the seeds, protected them, and fed them over time with water, warmth, and sunlight.

The promises of God are the same way. When you recognize a promise in God's Word that you want to see fulfilled in your life, then those are the promises to plant in your heart by faith. These promises are already true in the spirit, so all you have to do is trust them in your heart. Your trust plants that promise in your heart, and as you continue to believe, then you are drawing that promise into your soul by faith. To help you produce the fruit of this promise in your life, you can find a teacher to help you understand each promise you're believing with more clarity. Also, you can meditate on it throughout the day and ask the Holy Spirit to help you apply it to your life. This is a great way to see a harvest of God's Word come to pass in your life.

## Gardening Your Heart

God has entrusted you with a very important task! He has given you the task of being the Gardener of your heart. This is important because only you can determine how healthy the soil of your heart is and how much fruit you will produce for His kingdom. Your fruitfulness in God's Kingdom will depend upon your ability to steward the well-being of your heart.

---

**Your fruitfulness in God's Kingdom will depend upon your ability to steward the well-being of your heart.**

---

These simple steps will ensure that you are cultivating and protecting the seed of God's Word in the soil of your heart.

1. Plant the Word in your heart by believing it.
2. Continue in the Word by being a doer of the Word.
3. Cultivate your seeds and the soil of your heart through your relationship with God: reading and meditating on God's Word will continue to renew your mind to the things of God, and it will prepare the soil of your heart for all the good things He has planned for you.
4. Guard and protect the seeds in your heart by understanding the Word you've received, and by defending your heart from lies, offenses, cares, worldly lusts, and distractions. If you notice these types of rocks and weeds in your heart, immediately take them to God, and ask Him to help you gently remove these barriers from your heart.
5. The seed of the Word in your believing heart will automatically grow and bring forth fruit over time.
6. Harvest your fruit by continuing to live by the Word, glorifying God with your life, and letting others partake of the fruit that you produce! You will see the fruits of healing, prosperity, deliverance, provision,

and freedom spring forth in your life. Share your fruit with others by telling them your testimony and how they can receive the same freedom you've received.

There are thousands of specific promises in God's Word awaiting your discovery, so that you can plant them in your heart and walk them out in your daily life. Spend time with God praying over the promises that stand out to you, declare them over your life and your loved ones, and believe in your heart that you will see them come to pass.

Understanding the importance of God's Word caused me to prioritize it in my everyday life. I emphasized spending time with the Word so I would know the truth about God, the truth about myself, and the truth about others. I found that placing a priority on God's Word honored God, and as a result He honored me. Every area of my life overflowed with peace, joy, and blessing. Debts were released, finances increased, pains in my body were healed, my heart was restored, and my emotions were stable. My life overflowed with the truth: God is love and He loves me. Finally, I received the wholeness and completeness that God's Word promised me. I could taste, see, and feel the goodness of God in my life and I was becoming transformed through the Word of God!

These truths that I discovered about the Word of God will transform your life too! All you have to do is believe. Surrender your heart to Him and believe that the Word is truth. Then, prioritize it in your everyday life. God will show each step to take along the way. As a result of you honoring the Word of God, you will discover a life full of the blessing of God, the love of God, and the honor of God upon you.

> You will show me the way of life, granting me the joy of your presence and the pleasures of living with you forever. (Psalm 16:11)

# Transform Your Life

## Application of Chapter Concepts

### A Moment of Reflection: The Word of God

1. God's Word is your new mirror that you can align your life to. Evaluate your current belief system and compare it with the Word of God.
    - In what areas are you believing something that differs from the Word of God? How can you align your belief system to God's will for your life? For example: I did not know that God wants me healed. I would like to use my heart and words to confess God's truth over my body.

2. How is the soil of your heart doing? How can you be a better gardener of your heart? Write down your reflection in your journal.

3. What type of fruit do you see in your life today? What kind of fruit would you like to see?

- Write down some scriptures that contain promises that you would like to see come to pass in your life. Sow them in your heart by believing them, meditating on them, review them daily, and use your words to confess them over your life.

4. Let God know that you want to hear Him when He speaks to you.
    - Practice listening to God's voice by getting quiet and being alone with Him. Invite Him to lead you to scriptures to read and ask Him to speak to your heart. Write in your journal anything that you feel God is speaking to you.

5. Do you notice areas of your life where you need the power of God's Word to set you free from bondage and propel you into God's promises?
    - Find scriptures that align with God's truth and declare them over your situation.
    - For example:
        1. *Jesus bore my sins in His body on the cross; I am dead to sins, and alive to righteousness; by His stripes I was healed.* (1 Peter 2:24)

2. *Jesus became poor on the cross so that through His poverty I would be made rich.* (2 Corinthians 8:9)
3. *Jesus gave me a spirit of love, power, and a sound mind, so I resist fear, depression, and anxiety.* (2 Timothy 1:7)

6. Spend time alone with God, and let Him guide your heart. What is the next step of faith that you can take in these areas? What do you sense He is leading you to do next? Listen to His voice, and write down thoughts that come to your mind. Remember, God's voice will always agree with the Word. If a thought comes that contradicts God's Word, you can replace it with the truth.

## My Transformation Scripture

What is a scripture that speaks to you about the power of God's Word? Here are a few suggestions:
- For the word of God is alive and powerful. It is sharper than the sharpest two-edged sword, cutting between soul and spirit, between joint and marrow. It exposes our innermost thoughts and desires. (Hebrews 4:12)

- It is the same with my word. I send it out, and it always produces fruit. It will accomplish all I want it to, and it will prosper everywhere I send it. (Isaiah 55:11)
- Your word is a lamp to guide my feet and a light for my path. (Psalm 119:105)
- But if you look carefully into the perfect law that sets you free, and if you do what it says and don't forget what you heard, then God will bless you for doing it. (James 1:25)
- And you will know the truth, and the truth will set you free. (John 8:32)
- My child, pay attention to what I say. Listen carefully to my words. Don't lose sight of them. Let them penetrate deep into your heart, for they bring life to those who find them, and healing to their whole body. (Proverbs 4:20-22)

Write the scripture that you chose in your journal. Meditate on this verse throughout the day and remind yourself to protect this precious Word in your believing heart.

## Time in His Presence

Spend some time with God meditating on your transformation scripture. What do you think the Lord is speaking to you through this verse?

## Life Application

Ask Holy Spirit to help you apply this scripture to your daily life. How can I apply this to my life today?

## Prayer

If you acknowledge that the Word of God is truth, and that He has outlined His will for mankind through His Word, then please pray with me:

*Lord, thank You for revealing Your truth to me through Your Word. I acknowledge that Your Word is truth, and Your ways are better than my ways. I want to know You through Your Word; reveal Yourself to me and show me Your truth. I ask that You lead me, clean me, correct me, and teach me so that I bear fruit for Your kingdom. I open my heart to You through Your Word and Spirit. Show me how to make room for You in my daily life, so that I can bring Your will to pass in my life and the lives around me.*

*Thank You for every good thing that You're doing in my life. I love you, Father, Son, and Holy Spirit. In Jesus' mighty name I pray. Amen.*

# Chapter 5

## Is Your Mind a Bully?

### The Importance of a Happy, Healthy, Helpful Mind

*And now, dear brothers and sisters, one final thing. Fix your thoughts on what is true, and honorable, and right, and pure, and lovely, and admirable. Think about things that are excellent and worthy of praise.*
—Philippians 4:8

For most of my life, I was stuck in a cycle of negative thoughts toward God, toward myself, and toward others. Frankly, even as a Bible College student, I didn't know the importance of filtering and controlling my thoughts. As a result of my deception, I nearly ruined my relationship with my husband because I allowed myself to think so many negative thoughts about him. I feared that he was being unfaithful, and I allowed pains from my past to fuel my present. This created an inroad for Satan to steal from my life, my marriage, and my emotions. It was a horrible cycle and I thought that it was my husband's fault. I was deceived.

Praise God for His ability to speak to us and lead us through the Holy Spirit within us! Because of my habit of spending time with God every day, Holy Spirit got through to my heart and showed me that *I was the problem.* It wasn't fun to learn that I was wrong, but God's truth brought freedom to this area of my life. Once again, God's freedom led to fruit and transformation in my life, and in my marriage.

This makes me so grateful for God, the Bible, and the body of Christ. Spending time learning the truth about God's Word, getting it planted in my heart, and being surrounded with like-minded people who believe the same things has really helped me to understand the power of my mind. My teachers at Bible College and at church have helped me to see and realize that not all of my thoughts or emotions belong to me.

Is this a new concept to you as well?

Well, I hope you stick around to read the rest of this chapter, because when I understood this, I began to feed on positive thoughts instead of negative ones. This transformed my emotions and my self-image. It also changed the way I view other people and helped me to stop judgmental thoughts towards them. When I understood that not all of my thoughts are mine and that I need to filter the good ones from the bad ones, *I gained control of each area of my life through the power of my mind.* It flipped a switch inside of me that would no longer be bullied by self-demeaning thoughts, or be a bully by allowing rude thoughts towards others.

Controlling our thoughts is another spiritual principle formed by God that helps us to succeed and prosper. When we follow this and live by it, we enter into *even more* of God's promises and walk in greater freedom in our life. This is another way to prove the good, acceptable, and perfect will of God in your life!

> **Controlling our thoughts is another spiritual principle formed by God that helps us to succeed and prosper.**

## Think the Truth

I don't know about you, but I've noticed that my mind has a tendency to do what it wants to do! It can dream up far out and wild imaginations, and even conversations that have never happened. Before I know it, my emotions and heart are following suit and joining in on the conversation!

Take a moment to think about this with me. Have you ever had a conversation in your mind that has never happened? Maybe this dreamed-up conversation took a pretty quick turn, and suddenly, your heart is involved, beating faster, and your emotions are rising. Everything around you is normal, but inside, your mind took you on a journey that caused the chemicals in your body to respond and react. If you're not careful and you allow that conversation to keep going, it could cause you to respond in an irrational way.

God created us with the ability to imagine, dream, and direct the path of our life. These can also magnify or enlarge situations that may or may not be real. This is what the Bible refers to as meditation or imagination. The more you think about something or meditate on it, the more it will become enlarged in your life. The Bible says, "For as he *thinks* in his heart, so is he" (Proverbs 23:7a NKJV). What you think about is directly connected to the outcome of your life.

For example, I used to think that I was bad at managing my finances. That may have been true at the time, but the Bible says that God has given me the power to get wealth (Deut. 8:18). Therefore, that is truer than my inability to manage my finances in the natural. I sought out to align my natural situation with the spiritual truth. I searched the Bible for verses about finances, so I would know and understand the promises of God for this area of my life. I renewed my mind to the fact that God delights in my prosperity (Ps. 35:27), and I began to change the way that I thought. Whenever I had a negative thought about my finances, I would stop that thought and declare over myself, "God delights in my prosperity. I am a good steward of my finances. I pay off my debts quickly so that I am in debt to no man. I have a lot to give, and I am a cheerful giver. I abound and have abundance for every good work!"

The truth in God's Word taught me that my finances belong to God, and I am a steward of what He's given me. Over time, my actions, my heart, and my thoughts began to align with God's truth about my finances. Today, I give when God tells me to give, and I save and invest as God shows me to. Changing the way that I think about finances has changed the outcome of this area of my life. I am no longer in debt, I don't have to live paycheck to paycheck anymore, and I have way more than enough to give, tithe, and be a blessing to other people. I abound and have abundance for every good work! All of this happened because I aligned my mind, heart, and actions with God's truth. This example was for one area of my life, but God's Word is full of truth and wisdom for every area of the believer's life. If we can align our thinking to God's truth, then it can transform any area of our life.

Can you think of some negative thought patterns that you have? Maybe you do or maybe you don't. Either way, I encourage you develop the practice of monitoring your thoughts throughout the day. If you're able, take a note of any negative thoughts you discover. Instead of agreeing with every thought that you have, find out what the Bible says, and align your thoughts with His Word by replacing it with the truth. When in doubt, you can always follow this simple principle: think thoughts that are happy, healthy, and helpful—towards God, yourself, and others—and you'll be headed in the right direction!

> **Think thoughts that are happy, healthy, and helpful—towards God, yourself, and others—and you'll be headed in the right direction!**

# Change Your Thinking by Speaking

For a long time, I tried to stop negative thinking cold turkey and I didn't get very far. I would notice a thought that didn't align with God's truth, and I would try to think the thought away. *No! Go away, in Jesus' name!* To no avail, negative thoughts continued to come, and it was an exhausting battle. I wondered why this spiritual truth wasn't having any effect on my natural results. One day, I heard a Bible teacher speaking about the power of words. In the Bible, God and Jesus always created and transformed situations by speaking directly to the circumstance that they wanted to change. This is exactly what Jesus told us to do in

Mark 11:23 (NET). He said, "I tell you the truth, *if someone says to this mountain,* 'Be lifted up and thrown into the sea,' *and does not doubt in his heart but believes that what he says will happen,* it will be done for him." Whenever we try to remove a thought or a behavior from our life, it's important that we *replace* it by speaking the truth while believing in our heart. To emphasize this a little more, let's look at a couple translations of Philemon 1:6, which say:

> That the sharing of your faith may become effective **by the acknowledgment of every good thing which is in you in Christ Jesus.** (NKJV)

> I pray that the sharing of your faith may **become effective and powerful because of your accurate knowledge of every good thing which is ours in Christ.** (AMP)

This verse reminds me how important our thought patterns are. Thoughts can actually cause our faith to be more or less effective! Faith is *effective* and *powerful* when we acknowledge every good thing in us in Christ Jesus. When we acknowledge, recognize, and agree with God's Word in every situation, day by day, our faith is effective and powerful. The things that you speak forth with faith will come to pass. On the other hand, when we meditate on thoughts that don't align with God's truth, it limits the effect of our faith. The promises in God's Word that we're believing for can be hindered by our own thinking! Like Jesus said in Mark 11:23, if we speak to the mountain, such as a circumstance in life, while believing within our heart, then we will have what we speak.

The reason why we can't think bad thoughts away is because we are coming to a sword fight with a stick. When it comes to authority, our words have way more power than our thoughts do. Remember, God created all of creation with His Words—not thoughts. Jesus healed the sick, delivered demonic oppression, and accomplished great miracles through speaking—not through thinking. Of course, our thinking is involved, but that's not the source. The source of our power is in Christ, which is enforced through our words. When we need to gain spiritual ground and transform an area of our life so it aligns with God's truth, then we need to use the greatest source of authority we have: our voice.

> **The source of our power is in Christ, which is enforced through our words.**

This process helped me to stop negative thinking and align my thoughts with God's thoughts. It helped me to renew my mind to the truth, transform my life, and prove God's will in my life (Rom. 12:1-2). I follow this principle in my life each day because the atmosphere around me, my mind, and my heart, will follow the words that are coming out of my mouth.

You no longer have to think, *I'm sick. I'm poor. I'm depressed. I'm hopeless.* Because Jesus paid for you to have a prosperous, healed, blessed life. Every time you notice your thoughts going towards something negative, replace them and redirect them to the truth with your words. This will help you to *acknowledge* the truth of God's Word, and it will cause your faith to be powerful and effective. To help you align your words with God's Word, I have created a section in my *Walking in the New You! Workbook* with specific confessions you can declare over your life.

One of the biggest keys to walking in Christ's strength is to use your mind to work with you instead of against you! Once I understood this concept, it aligned every part of my soul (mind, will, emotions, and heart) with the truths in my spirit. This unlocked spiritual promises in my life that were being blocked from negative thoughts in my mind and beliefs in my heart. Aligning my thinking with my speaking helped my believing! It caused my faith to be effective and powerful, and it aligned my *whole* vessel, so that I could be fully committed to the things of God.

Don't allow negative thoughts to limit your faith any longer. Instead of agreeing with every thought that comes to your mind, stop them, and replace them by speaking the truth and believing in your heart. Use your mind to meditate on positive things that align with God's truth and that will magnify your faith and build you up. This simple switch will help you to renew your mind and align with God's promises, so that you can walk in freedom, transformation, and victory in every area of your life!

> For although we live in the natural realm, we don't wage a military campaign employing human weapons, using manipulation to achieve our aims. Instead, our spiritual weapons are energized with divine power to effectively dismantle the defenses behind which people hide. We can demolish every deceptive fantasy that opposes God and break through every arrogant attitude that is raised up in defiance of the true knowledge of God. **We capture, like prisoners of war, *every thought* and insist that it bow in obedience to the Anointed One.**
> (2 Corinthians 10:3-5 TPT)

# Transform Your Life

## Application of Chapter Concepts

### A Moment of Reflection: You Have the Mind of Christ

1. Do you recognize thoughts that are contrary to God's heart for you? If so, write down all the thoughts that you recognize. To take them captive, give those thoughts to Jesus, and ask the Father what truths you need to replace them with. Write down each truth that God gives you.

    - Every time you recognize a lie, use your words to stop that thought, and then confess the truth over yourself. Repeat this process as many times as you need to, until you see the victory in your life.

2. Spend time alone with God, and let Him guide your heart. What is the next step of faith that you can take in these areas? What do you sense He is leading you to do next? Listen to His voice, and write down thoughts that come to your mind. Remember, God's

voice will always agree with the Word. If a thought comes that contradicts God's Word, you can replace it with the truth.

## My Transformation Scripture

What is a scripture that speaks to you about the power of godly thoughts? Here are a few suggestions:

- You will keep in perfect peace all who trust in you, all whose thoughts are fixed on you! (Isaiah 26:3)
- So letting your sinful nature control your mind leads to death. But letting the Spirit control your mind leads to life and peace. (Romans 8:6)
- "My thoughts are nothing like your thoughts," says the LORD. "And my ways are far beyond anything you could imagine. For just as the heavens are higher than the earth, so my ways are higher than your ways and my thoughts higher than your thoughts." (Isaiah 55:8-9)
- Study this Book of Instruction continually. Meditate on it day and night so you will be sure to obey everything written in it. Only then will you prosper and succeed in all you do. (Joshua 1:8)
- O God, we meditate on your unfailing love as we worship in your Temple. (Psalm 48:9)

- "Who can know the LORD's thoughts? Who knows enough to teach him?" But we understand these things, for we have the mind of Christ.
(1 Corinthians 2:16)
- May the words of my mouth and the meditation of my heart be pleasing to you, O LORD, my rock and my redeemer. (Psalm 19:14)

Write the scripture that you chose in your journal. Meditate on this verse throughout the day, and remind yourself to stop negative thinking.

## Time in His Presence

Spend some time with God meditating on your transformation scripture. What do you think the Lord is speaking to you through this verse?

## Life Application

Ask Holy Spirit to help you apply this scripture to your daily life. How can I apply this to my life today?

## Prayer

If you acknowledge that God can transform your life as you align your thoughts with His thoughts, then please pray with me:

*Lord, thank You for giving me Your Word as a new mirror; a new, true lens through which I can view You, myself, and others. Help me to continually acknowledge all the good things within me in Christ Jesus, so that I glorify You in all that I do. I desire to grow and transform according to Your purpose for my life. To do so, I ask that You help me take captive destructive thinking that doesn't align with your truth, and replace it with thoughts that agree with You and Your Word. Thank You for Your help, God! In Jesus' name I pray. Amen.*

# Chapter 6

## Your Heart Matters

Encouraging Your Heart along the Path of Life

*For the eyes of the LORD run to and fro throughout the whole earth, to shew himself strong in the behalf of them whose heart is perfect toward him...*
—2 Chronicles 16:9a KJV

God knows the importance of our hearts, and He gives us a lot of instruction regarding it. He tells us how to garden it, to take care of it, guard it, protect it, and to love Him with it.

Your heart is the source of your life. It is connected to everything that you do. Your heart is also the only part of you that is directly connected to your spirit. Your heart unites your soul and spirit. Therefore, it has the ability to bring the promises within your spirit into your soul, body, and every sphere of your life. Just as if your heart were to stop beating, then your life would stop, so it is that if your heart stops believing, then your spiritual life would stop. Believing in your heart is how you become born again. Before that time, you were spiritually dead. Your believing heart is how you enter into all the life and promises of God initially, and it's how you continue to enter into the fullness of God.

Once again, if I would have understood this earlier, then I would have been a better steward of my heart. It would have saved me from a lot of loss, pain, and disappointment. But, because I decided to give God all of my heart in the very beginning, it also saved me from a lot of misfortune.

God can do amazing, unlimited things in the life of a believing, surrendered heart.

# A Believing Heart

Did you know that your faith can be dormant and ineffective? Five times in the gospels, Jesus corrects people for having little faith (Matt. 6:30, 8:26, 14:31, 16:8; Luke 12:28). In these verses, [1]the Greek translation for *O ye of little faith* means incredulous and lacking confidence. [2]The definition of *incredulous* means unwilling to admit or accept what is offered as true. This means that we can hear the truth and be *unwilling* to accept it in our hearts. Where does willingness begin? God has given all of us the freedom of free will or choice, and it all begins in our hearts. That is our source of life, our source of choice, and what guides our lives.

This tells me that even if I have faith, it doesn't mean that I'm using it effectively. You could be using your faith to believe God for great things, which is awesome! Or your faith may be dormant and ineffective because your heart is unbelieving. Maybe you believe God in some areas of your life, but in other areas you don't believe. If that's so, then you are missing out on a lot of *good things* in your life. This is why the Bible tells you in several places *to trust God with all of your heart* (Prov. 3:5), *seek God with all of your heart* (Jer. 29:13), and *love God with all of your heart* (Mark 12:30). If you can trust, seek, and love God with all of your heart, then you can also trust, seek, and love God with only part of your heart. When God only has part of your heart, then you can only use part of your faith.

> For it is by believing in your heart that you are made right with God, and it is by openly declaring your faith that you are saved. (Romans 10:10)

A believing heart is how you become saved and enter into God's promise of eternal salvation. A believing heart is how you continue to walk in the rest of God's promises (Col. 2:6-7). If you only believe some parts of the Bible and not others, then your faith will be little, or ineffective. If you believe that the Word of God can be used to help you, equip you, and prepare you for every good opportunity in life, then your entire spirit, soul, and body will be filled, full, and overflowing with the blessing of God. Romans 4:20 says, "Abraham never wavered in believing God's promise. In fact, his faith grew stronger, and in this he brought glory to God." A believing heart causes your faith to be strong, active, and effective. It causes you to enter into the things God has promised you and planned for you.

> A believing heart causes your faith to be strong, active, and effective. It causes you to enter into the things God has promised you and planned for you.

## Assure Your Heart in the Love and Goodness of God

Life is full of trials and tribulations that can mark your life forever. Your heart and mind will try to condemn you along the way and tell you to give up. Your emotions will scream at you and your thoughts will come against you. In these moments, you will need to encourage yourself in the truth. You will need the love of God as an anchor for your soul (Heb. 6:19).

1 John 3:18-19 says,

> Little children, let us not love in word or talk but in deed and in truth. By this we shall know that we are of the truth and **reassure our heart before him** (NKJV).

Knowing the love of God will reassure your heart along the path of your life journey. God's love will anchor your heart and give you the ability to walk out God's truth in your daily life.

We see this ability to encourage and assure our hearts displayed in the life of David. In 1 Samuel 30:1-6, David and his people were going through a hard time. Their city had just been burned, and all the wives and children had just been taken captive.

It says in 1 Samuel 30:4-6a,

> They wept until they could weep no more. David's two wives...were among those captured. David was now in great danger because all his men were very bitter about losing their sons and daughters, and they began to talk of stoning him...

What a horrible situation! Everyone and everything had turned against David. His own men wanted to kill him and were about to stone him. It looked as if all was lost. But look at how David responded to this situation.

> ... But David encouraged himself in the Lord his God. (1 Samuel 30:6b KJV)

David could have quit and given up, but instead he encouraged his own heart in the Lord! David knew that despite these life and death circumstances that God is faithful and that His love is true.

Just like David, we need the ability to assure our hearts and encourage ourselves in the Lord when everything else is coming against us. How do we do this? True strength can only be found in the love and truth of God. A firm foundation in the love and truth of God will anchor our souls and strengthen us when the battle gets hot.

> **A firm foundation in the love and truth of God will anchor our souls and strengthen us when the battle gets hot.**

What was the result of this *inner strengthening* that David received? The story goes on to tell you that David sought God's direction and asked Him what to do. This is so important for us as well. When we seek God, He will always give us direction. God told David to pursue the army that had taken their wives and children, and they did. And look at what happened in 1 Samuel 30:18-19. It says, "David got back everything the Amalekites had taken, and he rescued his two wives. Nothing was missing: small or great, son or daughter, nor anything else that had been taken. **David brought everything back."**

Through David's ability to encourage himself in the Lord, he strengthened himself to keep going. David quieted his emotions and the noise around him so he could focus his attention on God instead of the circumstances. This realigned his heart and mind back on the Lord, and he received the direction he needed to redeem the situation. This not only benefited David, but he *recovered all* for all of his people. Everything that was lost had been restored, and they even received additional spoil from the camp of the enemy (vv 20).

I practice this same principle in my everyday life. Every day, I experience emotions, thoughts, and sometimes even circumstances that seem contrary to God's goodness and truth in my life. My thoughts try to tell me, *you're not good enough, you're not going to finish this project, who do you think you are, you're not going to succeed in this.* Over and over, day by day the soundtrack plays. There may not be an army of men that wants to stone me, and I may not have my family and home taken from me, but sometimes it feels that way.

Life has a tendency to come against you, right? What do you do in these types of situations? Do you talk yourself through them and comfort yourself? Do you assure your heart that God is for you and regardless of what your heart is trying to tell you, you know that you're headed in the right direction? Whether it's your own thoughts coming against you, or your heart condemning your every action, there is a need to resist the negative and enforce the positive.

For example, I'm passionate about living a healthy lifestyle. In the beginning of my faith and fitness journey, I used to feel condemned if I didn't work out or eat healthy every day. This caused me to feel exhausted and burdened by the goals that I set for myself. Instead of pursuing this passion from a place of joy and contentment, I was pressuring myself to perform so that I could look a certain way. The Bible tells us that comparing ourselves with one another is unwise (2 Cor. 10:12). Over time, this truth began to sink in. When I stopped trying to "perform" in order to get results and started "doing" from Christ's strength and identity within me, it became effortless for me to maintain a healthy lifestyle. I saw myself *in Christ*, and when guilt or condemnation tried to come against me, I resisted it, confident in Christ—not in my actions.

These silly types of condemnation will try to come against you in every area of your life; telling you that you are falling short: always failing, and never succeeding. That's not true when you get born again because you are identical to Christ in *this lifetime!* The Scripture says, **"...because as he is so also are we in this world"** (1 John 4:17 ESV).

This is why we need to assure our hearts in God's love and truth. No one is perfect, and our actions will never be perfect. God isn't asking for perfection from us because Jesus was perfect for us. God is only looking for a willing heart and a surrendered life. Remembering these things will help our hearts to stay encouraged throughout our journey of faith. It will help us to love, accept, and forgive others when they are having a hard day. When someone does or says something that was hurtful, we can still show love towards them, and encourage them on their path. This outlook will help us to anchor our hearts in God's love so that we aren't relying on outward circumstances to bring stability to our life. Our hearts will not find the stability we need through life's circumstances. Nor will we find it in our own actions, or in the actions and approval of others. Stability (inward and outward) can only come from one place: God's love.

If you know that God loves you unconditionally, then you will be able to show that same love towards the people around you despite their performance. Even on days when you, or the people around you, miss the mark, you can rest in the love of God and find shelter in His mighty wings. Because of Christ in you, you can encourage your heart, knowing that you are headed in the right direction. From there, you can approach the throne of God with boldness and confidence; quiet your mind, heart, and emotions, and guide them back to the truth. This simple practice will give your heart (your life source) strength and encouragement to keep going. This will give you the direction you need to recover what's been lost, and gather the abundance God intended your life to have.

## Open Your Heart to God

We have control over our hearts, which gives us the ability to either believe God or disbelieve God.

Be careful then, dear brothers and sisters. Make sure that your own hearts are not evil and unbelieving, turning you away from the living God. You must warn each other every day, while it is still "today," so that none of you will be deceived by sin and hardened against God. For if we are faithful to the end, trusting God just as firmly as when we first believed, we will share in all that belongs to Christ. Remember what it says: "Today when you hear his voice, don't harden your hearts as Israel did when they rebelled." (Hebrews 3:12-15)

In these verses, we see that the author is telling us, "Make sure that your own hearts are not evil and unbelieving, turning you away from the living God" (vv 12). When we choose not to believe God and the Bible, we are choosing evil, and it turns us away from God instead of towards God. This hardens our heart against God, and opens us up to sin and deception, and creates an inroad for Satan to steal from our lives. On the contrary, when God speaks to you, open your heart to Him and believe Him. This will cause you to enter His promises and "all that belongs to Christ" (vv 14). When God reveals truth to us, we have the choice to believe Him, trust Him, and respond in faith.

How can we make sure that we are believing the truth when we hear it? By spending time with God, being intentional to give Him all of our heart, and meditating on the things He's showing us. Spending time in His presence with the Word and the Holy Spirit softens our heart. This gives God time and space to root these truths in our heart, so we can walk them out in our daily life.

## All of Your Heart

I remember sitting on my bed one Saturday morning, reading and thinking about God's Word. I was reading Proverbs 3:5-6, which says,

> Trust in the LORD with all your heart; do not depend on your own understanding. Seek his will in all you do, and he will show you which path to take.

I remember reading that verse and asking myself, "Do I really trust God with *all* of my heart?" At that time, my answer was "no." I was still holding on to areas of my heart that I hadn't given to God. Specifically, in the areas of believing God for a husband, and receiving promotions at work, I was trusting in myself and my ability to get results instead of God. As a result, He was limited in how He could speak to me and lead me. In that moment, God revealed to me that these verses were connected. First, I have to trust in the Lord *with all of my heart,* and *then I will be able to depend on God and His understanding* instead of my own. Then, I can seek His will in everything I do, and He can show me the path to take. If God doesn't have *all* of my heart trusting Him, then I can't have His understanding, His will in my life, or His guidance. God needs all of my heart, so that I can have His help and wisdom. Trust me, I need His help and wisdom to go anywhere in life!

I believe that these little moments are divine interventions, when we take time to pull away from the world and life and the busyness, and we are intentional to get quiet and be with Him. This is what He needs to speak to our hearts.

I love the relationship that the Psalmists had with God. Throughout the Psalms, I see heartache, love, pain, distrust, trust, and a plethora of life situations and emotions that I can relate to. The Psalmists may not have always had it "right," but they were headed in the right direction. Their heart was for God and despite everything they felt and experienced, they continually turned back to God, trying to weigh their heart and emotions with the truth. In Psalm 4:4-5 it says,

Tremble, and do not sin; meditate in your heart upon your bed, and be still. Selah. Offer the sacrifices of righteousness, and trust in the LORD. (NASB)

The author of this Psalm knew the power of being quiet, meditating with your heart on your bed, and getting still with God. This simple act is a sweet aroma; a sacrifice of righteousness to the Lord. When you take time to do this, it displays your trust in the Lord to turn to Him each day to seek His heart. This gives God the ability to soften your heart, give you wisdom, and show you the path to take. God's ways and His path will always lead you to success, freedom, peace, and joy.

> **God's ways and His path will always lead you to success, freedom, peace, and joy.**

# Discerning God's Direction

When God speaks to your heart, it will feel like enlightenment, clarity, or fresh air within you. Suddenly, you will understand how God is speaking to you through His Word. That is God shining the light of His wisdom on your heart and situation, and He will show you the path to take. You will have an inner knowing of whether you should keep going or change directions. On the other hand, if you recognize guilt, shame, negative thoughts, or condemnation coming against you, that is not how God speaks to you. This is when you need to assure your heart with the truth that God loves you and that you are headed in the right direction. God will never be harsh towards you or condemning. God is pleased with you. You are His beloved child, and He is not angry or disappointed with you.

God may bring correction as a loving Father would, but it will never be in the voice of condemnation (Rom. 8:1). When God corrects you, it will feel like conviction. Conviction is when your heart bears witness to the truth, and the Holy Spirit will show you, "this is the truth; walk in it" (Is. 30:21). Suddenly, you know that what you're doing doesn't align with God's will for your life. In those moments, you have an opportunity to obey and yield to God. If you do, you will go deeper and further in your walk with Him. If you do not, it will harden your heart towards Him, and it opens the door for Satan to steal from your life. When God reveals truth to your heart, it is your choice and responsibility to believe and obey Him. If God gives you a step to take, He will not give you another step until you fulfill the first step.

Obeying these quiet, inner enlightenments is how you walk out being a living sacrifice and yielding every area of your life to God. As you do so, you will mature and grow in the Christian walk. Over time, it will become easier for you to discern when God is leading you, and it will become easier. Your life will be set apart for God's glory, and you will walk in more and more freedom.

> **Obeying these quiet, inner enlightenments is how you walk out being a living sacrifice and yielding every area of your life to God.**

# Waiting for the Promise

God has healed me and restored every area of my life, step by step, through an open, surrendered heart. After drug addiction, I decided that I knew nothing, and that I needed the wisdom of God to lead me. That was the smartest decision I've ever made, and I have never regretted it. Giving God all of my heart has helped me to be a true living sacrifice, which has caused me to surrender every area of my life to His care.

This decision to give God all of my heart has helped me to give God my plans, my will, my desires, and my way of doing things. It's helped me to trust Him with all of my heart because He knows better than I do.

Sometimes, doors that I wanted to open would close right in front of my face. I thought *this job promotion would be perfect for me,* but the door would close. Or I thought a certain man would be a great husband, but the door would close. Times like that don't always feel good, and I would wonder if I was doing the right thing. In those moments, I'd have to decide whether I would yield to God or try to pry the door open on my own. As a drug addict, I was so familiar with making my own way. Like a bull in a China shop, I would force my will upon others and create my own doors so I could walk through them. History proves that "doing it my way" only causes more hurt, heartache, and chaos. In the Bible, this is how Ishmael was born before Isaac in Genesis 16. Abram and Sarai were tired of waiting for God's promise, so they went outside of God's will and created the promise on their own. Whenever we do this, we are exalting our will above God's will and creating a curse instead of a promise. We cannot force God's promises to come to pass—we must plant them in our hearts and wait for them to blossom.

So, when the door closed in my face, I would run to my secret place with God, cry in His lap, give Him my heart, and let Him comfort me through those times. The Bible says that He would give me the desires of my heart if I trusted Him and committed them to Him (Ps. 37:3-5). Hanging on to that promise, regardless of how I felt, I would continue to trust Him and encourage my heart in the Lord. I knew that if God was my loving Father, and if His Word was true, then when it's His will and timing, that God Himself will open the right doors for me to walk through. While I waited for these desires in my heart to come to pass, I trusted Him with all of my heart, continued to seek Him with all of my heart, and kept loving Him with all of my heart. In the waiting, I found the strength and the encouragement my heart needed, plus a deeper, more intimate relationship with God.

Eventually, the right doors opened, and all the desires of my heart have been fulfilled, or are being fulfilled. Simple things like living arrangements, financial breakthrough, healing, having a godly friend group, promotions at work, and even a husband! God opened these doors for me through my waiting, trusting heart. When I finally stopped trying to control certain areas of my life, He was truly able to lead me to His fullness and goodness. I began to prove the good, acceptable, and perfect will of God in my life (Rom. 12:2).

God cares about all of these details in your life, too. If you give God all of your heart and every area of your life today, you will never, ever regret it. Life with God is full of blessing, fun, and adventure. Giving Him all of your heart is the key that will unlock untold blessings and promises in your life. He will not only lead you to the desires in your heart, but if you wait for Him to open the right doors, He will open far better doors than you could even think or imagine. God's promises are worth waiting for!

> **Giving Him all of your heart is the key that will unlock untold blessing and promises in your life.**

I would have lost heart, unless I had believed that I would see the goodness of the LORD in the land of the living. Wait on the LORD; be of good courage, and He shall strengthen your heart; wait, I say, on the LORD! (Psalm 27:13-14 NKJV)

The small matters of the heart are a key to unlock the door of God's goodness and fullness. Your believing heart can unlock the promises of God's Word simply by believing. Through His Word, God tells us to trust Him with all our heart (Prov. 3:5), seek Him with all of our heart (Jer. 29:13), and love Him with all of our heart (Mark 12:30). No matter what trials come against you in life, you will be able to assure your heart in the goodness and truth of God, which will strengthen you to finish your course full of faith. Your heart is the precious part of you that can connect and commune with God, hear His direction and encouragement, equipping you to take action full of the wisdom and power of God. If God has all of your heart, then He has every area of your life and He will be able to lead your life into wholeness, freedom, and victory.

# Transform Your Life

## Application of Chapter Concepts

### A Moment of Reflection: Your Heart Is Important

1. Do you recognize any areas of your life where you aren't believing God? How can you open your heart to Him and trust Him more?
   - Ask God to help you trust Him, and tell Him why it's hard for you. It's ok to be honest with God—He will not be mad at you, but He will be able to reveal Himself to you the more honest you are with Him.
   - Write these things down in your journal.

2. In what areas of your life are you ready to give God all of your heart?
   - Take note of these areas in your journal.
   - What are you believing God to do in these areas of your life?

3. Are you waiting for God's promises to come to pass in your life?
   - God can do more than you think, ask, or imagine in every area of your life. Waiting for God's will to come to pass is always worth the wait. Let God know that you desire His will in your life. Write down every area where you will wait for Him, and believe to see His promises come to pass.

4. Spend time alone with God, and let Him guide your heart. What is the next step of faith that you can take in these areas? What do you sense He is leading you to do next? Listen to His voice, and write down thoughts that come to your mind. Remember, God's voice will always agree with the Word. If a thought comes that contradicts God's Word, you can replace it with the truth.

## My Transformation Scripture

What is a scripture that speaks to you about the importance of your heart? Here are a few suggestions:
- The eyes of the LORD search the whole earth in order to strengthen those whose hearts are fully

committed to him. (2 Chronicles 16:9a)
- Guard your heart above all else, for it determines the course of your life. (Proverbs 4:23)
- Let the words of my mouth and the meditation of my heart be acceptable in Your sight, O LORD, my strength and my Redeemer. (Psalm 19:14 NKJV)
- Be angry, and do not sin. Meditate within your heart on your bed, and be still. *Selah.* (Psalm 4:4 NKJV)
- But they delight in the law of the LORD, meditating on it day and night. They are like trees planted along the riverbank, bearing fruit each season. Their leaves never wither, and they prosper in all they do. (Psalm 1:2-3)
- Trust in the LORD with all your heart; do not depend on your own understanding. Seek his will in all you do, and he will show you which path to take. (Proverbs 3:5-6)
- Who may ascend onto the hill of the LORD? And who may stand in His holy place? One who has clean hands and a pure heart, who has not lifted up his soul to deceit and has not sworn deceitfully. He will receive a blessing from the LORD and righteousness from the God of his salvation. (Psalm 24:3-5)

Write the scripture that you chose in your journal. Meditate on this verse throughout the day and remind yourself to align your heart with God's heart.

## Time in His Presence

Spend some time with God meditating on your transformation scripture. What do you think the Lord is speaking to you through this verse?

## Life Application

Ask Holy Spirit to help you apply this scripture to your daily life. How can I apply this to my life today?

## Prayer

If you acknowledge the power of your believing heart to bring forth the promises of God's Word, then please pray with me:

*Lord, thank You for giving me a new heart and a new life in Christ. I recognize the power of my heart, and I ask that You help me to align my heart with Your heart in every way. Thank You for equipping me with Your Word and Your Spirit to live the victorious life of Christ. In Jesus' name I pray. Amen."*

# Chapter 7

# A Relationship of Trust

Trusting God to Finish the Work He Started in You

*And I am certain that God, who began the good work within you, will continue his work until it is finally finished on the day when Christ Jesus returns.*
—Philippians 1:6

Once I learned how to truly give my heart, my mind, my words, and my life to God, I was fully ready to be "all in for God." There was no more straddling the world and my faith. It was everything or nothing.

I knew that my **spirit** had been made perfect in Christ, I was applying those truths to my **soul** (mind, will, emotions), and now it was time to let these truths overflow into my **body** and every area of my life. I could discern the difference between right and wrong, and I understood the Bible enough to apply it to my life. From this point on, God was giving me a choice. I could apply what I was learning to my life *each day*—or not. If I chose to move forward with God and do the things that He was asking me to do, then my entire life would change. My natural life would transform into the entirely new creation that I already was in my spirit, and I would reflect the image of God more and more in my everyday life. Layers of my old life would be peeled away as God molded me into the person He created me to be. But He never forced me...not once. Sometimes it hurt so bad as I clearly faced the internal struggle between God's will and my will, the *new way* of life or *my way* of life. God gave me a choice from the beginning, and every time I said, "yes," to His ways, I went deeper and deeper into His purpose and plan for my life.

I'm so glad that He gives me grace to do the things He's called me to do. Without His strength, courage, and ability within me, I would never be able to succeed in these things. I would fall flat on my face, and run away in fear—which I tried to do many times. A trusting reliance upon God not only equips you to succeed, but it also prevents burnout, disappointment, and discouragement in the midst of life's circumstances.

Whenever God asks you to do something, He is giving you an opportunity to trust Him. Every time you choose to trust Him, He will always reveal His power, strength, and ability to work on your behalf. God will always prove His faithfulness and goodness to you when you trust Him.

# God's Proposal to You

The entire Christian walk is a choice. Salvation is a choice. Consider the desires in your heart as a choice: a proposal from God. He is not forcing you to follow His direction, but when you do, it will always lead to a more abundant life. Deuteronomy 30:19 says, "I call heaven and earth as witnesses today against you, that I have set before you life and death, blessing and cursing; therefore choose life, that both you and your descendants may live." God's way will always lead to a life of blessing.

God is proposing to you to invite you into a relationship, a partnership where you trust Him more than you trust anyone else. God wants to partner with you in your life, so that in everything, no matter how great or small, you can trust Him. You must first learn to trust Him with the small things, so that you can eventually trust Him with great things. Each proposal that He presents to you is a steppingstone to lead you to your destiny. God knows exactly how to lead you to the people and places that will recognize your gifts and sharpen your talents and abilities. God's proposal to you is to prepare you for where He's destined you to be. One day at a time, you surrender to His direction. Several years later you are going to look back and see how God has shaped your life perfectly!

---

**God wants to partner with you in your life, so that in everything, no matter how great or small, you can trust Him.**

God is not leading you to make life hard on you. However, that doesn't mean it's always going to feel easy. Your flesh may want to run the other direction. It might stretch you and pull you out of your comfort zone, which is good. This is how growth happens!

## Trust

Your ability to trust God and rely on your relationship with Him will enable you to make decisions of faith that you were never able to make before. Many times in my life, God has led me by my conscience. It felt like that internal knowing of right and wrong. I knew that God was telling me to do something, but it seemed impossible.

> **Your ability to trust God and rely on your relationship with Him, will enable you to make decisions of faith that you were never able to make before.**

In my own ability, it appeared as if God was asking me to climb Mt. Everest. I would look at that mountainous request from God and run away cowering in fear of my weakness and inability. But all He was asking for was my trust. It was as if God encouraged me by saying, "Trust Me, and I will accomplish the impossible in your life." So I would take one small, shaking step of faith, trembling in my boots. And He would meet me there—at my point of faith. So I would take another small, searching step, wondering if I would fall flat on my face. And He would meet me there. Every time that I took a step, even if it was miserable in my own eyes, it was great in His eyes. All I needed to do was trust Him. Rely on my relationship with Him. Give Him all of my heart, and trust that He is good and true.

As a result, 100 small, shaky steps turned into several years of God doing the impossible in my life. He taught me that He will never fail me. That He will always be here for me. Even when it hurts and looks like my life has fallen apart again, God is still there—strong, mighty, and faithful on my behalf. The same God that has been faithful to me, will be mighty, strong, and faithful to you. All He is asking for is for you to trust Him.

> **One hundred small, shaky steps turned into several years of God doing the impossible in my life.**

Several stories in the Bible remind me of how I've felt in my own walk with God. One example is Moses. God was asking this man to lead millions of Israelites out of bondage and into the promised land. I can only imagine how Moses must have felt. The story is laid out for you in Exodus chapter 4. Moses gave God one excuse after another, explaining to God why he was the wrong person to use. But God continued to meet Moses's excuses with God's ability. Finally, in Exodus chapter 6, you discover whose ability is going to accomplish this mountainous quest. As you read, pay attention to how many times God says, "I will."

Exodus 6:6-8 says,

> Therefore say to the children of Israel: "I am the LORD; **I will** bring you out from under the burdens of the Egyptians, **I will** rescue you from their bondage, and **I will** redeem you with an outstretched arm and with great judgments. **I will** take you as My people, and **I will** be your God. Then you shall know that I am the LORD your God who brings you out from under the burdens of the Egyptians. And **I will** bring you into the land which I swore to give to Abraham, Isaac, and Jacob; and **I will** give it to you as a heritage: I am the LORD."

God told Moses, you don't have to do anything but trust me and do what I tell you to do. I believe that God is telling you the same thing today. As a result, **God will** do for you the same things He did for Moses, and the same things He did for me. **God will:**

- Deliver you from every burden that's weighing you down
- Rescue you from bondage
- Redeem and vindicate you
- Give you a new identity in the family of God
- Bring you into a better relationship with God
- Bring you into your promised land
- Give you eternal inheritance and purpose

The only choice you have to make is to trust God every step of the way. Your relationship with God will carry you through every situation in life, and help you to climb even the tallest mountains. On the other side of the mountain, you will discover a life that is set free from bondage, a life that is redeemed and delivered from anything that has been holding you back. This type of freedom gives you access to run further, fly higher, and accomplish even more impossible things with God! Nothing is impossible for those who will believe and trust Him (Luke 1:37).

> **On the other side of the mountain, you will discover a life that is set free from bondage, a life that is redeemed and delivered from anything that has been holding you back.**

## The Pruning Process

Most Christians don't start their walk of faith producing a hundredfold fruit from the Word of God. It is encouraging to know that it's not a contest, and that God is pleased with you right where you are. However, He loves you enough to not leave you where you are! God knows your potential in Christ and He wants to continue to see you grow and bring forth fruit for His kingdom. The more fruit you produce, the more the Father is glorified by your life, and the more He can use you to bring heaven to earth. God wants to bless your life and fill your life with His promises, but He also wants to use the blessings in your life so you can be a blessing to others.

Let's read John 15:1-8 together:

I am the true vine, and My Father is the vine-dresser. Every branch in Me that does not bear fruit He takes away; and every branch that bears fruit He prunes, that it may bear more fruit. You are already clean because of the word which I have spoken to you. Abide in Me, and I in you. As the branch cannot bear fruit of itself, unless it abides in the vine, neither can you, unless you abide in Me. I am the vine, you are the branches. He who abides in Me, and I in him, bears much fruit; for without Me you can do nothing. If anyone does not abide in Me, he is cast out as a branch and is withered; and they gather them and throw them into the fire, and they are burned. If you abide in Me, and My words abide in you, you will ask what you desire, and it shall be done for you. By this My Father is glorified, that you bear much fruit; so you will be My disciples.

You can see from this passage that the Father's heart is for you to abide in Him so that you bring forth His fruit.

**Being fruitful is manifesting the promises of God in your life.** When you are bearing God's fruit in your life, you are proving that the Word of God is true, that God is who He says He is, and He is glorified by your life! Bearing fruit is proving that there is healing, deliverance, salvation, freedom, joy, and wealth for everyone who believes in Christ!

You cannot bring forth fruit unless you are abiding (living, dwelling, remaining) in Christ. Then, when you bear fruit, He will prune you so you can bring forth even more fruit! When you don't abide in Christ, you do not bring forth fruit, and you are discarded as a fruitless branch. Remaining in the Word of God in every season of life will ensure that you are abiding in Christ, and bringing forth fruit for His kingdom.

> My son, keep thy fathers commandment, and forsake not the law of thy mother: Bind them continually upon thine heart, and tie them about thy neck. When thou goest, it shall lead thee; when thou sleepest, it shall keep thee; and when thou awakest, it shall talk with thee. For the commandment is a lamp; and the law is light; and reproofs of instruction are the way of life. (Proverbs 6:20-23 KJV)

> **Be encouraged whenever you receive correction from God because He loves you, and He wants to increase your potential in life through His goodness!**

Not many people like the word "instruction" or "correction." However, God is a loving Father, and He only prunes and corrects the ones He loves (Prov. 3:12). As you spend time in the Word, the Lord will reveal Himself to you, love you, speak to you, guide you, and correct you. Be encouraged whenever you receive correction from God because He loves you, and He wants to increase your potential in life through His goodness! As a loving Father, God's goal is to add value to your life through His divine counsel and leadership. God will not correct you through harshness or anger, but He will draw you with His loving presence, and reveal His best to you through His Word and Spirit.

> And that from a child thou hast known the holy scriptures, which are able to make thee wise unto salvation through faith which is in Christ Jesus. All scripture is given by inspiration of God, and is profitable for doctrine, for reproof, for correction,

for instruction in righteousness: that the man of God may be perfect, thoroughly furnished unto all good works. (2 Timothy 3:15-17 KJV)

The Bible is a gift from God to mankind. God will use His Word to clean and prune every area of your life so you can bear more fruit, and become perfected and equipped for every good work.

## The Onion Principle

Your life has layers and layers and layers—like an onion. God needs you to give Him time and space so He can peel back the layers that need removed. That's how He gets to the fruit! If God told you everything that needed to change about you and your life all at once, it would hurt you severely. That's why you must practice submitting to God each day. Give Him some of your time every day, so that He can speak to you, love you, reveal your strengths to you, and lead you to your purpose on the earth. He will also lovingly disclose things about your life that disagree with His nature and character so that you can look more like your Father. Every child wants to be just like their parents. If you have a correct image of God, then you would want to be just like Him. He wants to reveal the truth to you about who He is, so that you can shine with goodness and glory.

When I was a drug addict, I was a full-time drug addict for seven years. Meaning, I was good at being a drug addict. That's all that I did, and my life was corrupt with ungodliness. I did not have any healthy habits, and I hated anything and everything that was good for me. I remember when I was two years into my recovery from drug addiction and my roommate asked me, "Do you want to go to the gym with me?" I literally scoffed and laughed out loud before I said, "No!" At that time, I despised the idea of working out. I ate fast food every day, smoked cigarettes professionally, cussed like a sailor, and I thought I had life figured out. Well, I was still sober and I loved God, but it took time for me to renew my mind to the ways of God.

For years, God was removing layers of ungodliness from my life. Even though it wasn't always easy, I became raptured by the love of God; enveloped by His presence in my room, day after day after day, alone with Him, but completely content and satisfied. I became so in love with God that all I wanted to do was to be with Him. Even in my early twenties, I would rather be alone with God, reading His Word, enjoying my time with Him, than being out with friends or watching movies.

My roommate would ask me if I wanted to watch a movie, and I remember the feeling I would get. It was like inside, Holy Spirit was drawing me, wooing me with His love and gentleness saying, "Come, be with me." Sometimes I would listen, and sometimes I didn't. Sometimes, I would resist Holy Spirit, and want to watch a movie. But, after a few minutes, I couldn't stand the feeling of telling Him, "no," and I would go back to my room to be with Him. Being in the presence of God is always far more satisfying than any temptation the flesh can offer.

> **Being in the presence of God is always far more satisfying than any temptation the flesh can offer.**

...Rise up, my love, my fair one, and come away! (Song of Solomon 2:13 NKJV)

Being in the presence of God is how you restore your life to the ways and will of God. As you renew your mind with the Word, every other area of your life will change, layer by layer. The old life with its old ways will be peeled away so that the new life can break through. Over time, you will recognize God's love and kindness helping you, and the transformation that can take place with consistent time in His presence.

The ability to trust God in the midst of daily life is critical in the life of the believer. Trust is how you submit to God and resist the devil so that he flees (James 4:7). Trusting God with all of your heart is how you rely on God's wisdom instead of your own understanding (Pro. 3:5). As you practice trusting God in your daily life, you will be led forth with peace and quiet assurance. Your decisions will be met with the favor of God and man, and success will be around every corner. Trusting God is how you collide with prosperity in every area of your life. The person who trusts God will not fail.

Even when it's hard and when it hurts, your relationship with God will carry you through the journey. It may feel uncomfortable, but always remember this: God's not leading you to your death; He's leading you to success!

# Transform Your Life

## Application of Chapter Concepts

### A Moment of Reflection: Trust Leads to Transformation

1. Is God asking you to do something, by faith, that requires you to trust Him? If so, what is it?
   - Ask God, "What scripture can I stand on during this season?"
     1. This scripture can be like a compass to guide you, encourage you, and help you trust the promise of God's Word in this season.
     2. What would you like to see God do in this season of your life?
     3. Write these things down in your journal so that you can review them.

2. Do you sense that God is pruning you, or removing old layers that need to be removed from your life?

What area is He pruning? How can you cooperate with God during this time?

- If so, congratulations! It's an honor and a privilege for God to restore your life from the inside out. This is part of the powerful process of transformation, and God is faithful to finish the good work He's started in you.

3. Spend time alone with God, and let Him guide your heart. What is the next step of faith that you can take in these areas? What do you sense He is leading you to do next? Listen to His voice, and write down thoughts that come to your mind. Remember, God's voice will always agree with the Word. If a thought comes that contradicts God's Word, you can replace it with the truth.

## My Transformation Scripture

What is a scripture that speaks to you about the power of trusting in God? Here are a few suggestions:

- So if you are suffering in a manner that pleases God, keep on doing what is right, and trust your lives to the God who created you, for he will never fail you. (1 Peter 4:19)

- For this reason I also suffer these things; nevertheless I am not ashamed, for I know whom I have believed and am persuaded that He is able to keep what I have committed to Him until that Day. (2 Tim. 1:12 NKJV)
- Trust in the LORD and do good. Then you will live safely in the land and prosper. Take delight in the LORD, and he will give you your heart's desires. Commit everything you do to the LORD. Trust him, and he will help you. He will make your innocence radiate like the dawn, and the justice of your cause will shine like the noonday sun. (Psalm 37:3-6.)
- Many sorrows come to the wicked, but unfailing love surrounds those who trust the LORD. (Psalm 32:10)
- But let all who take refuge in you rejoice; let them sing joyful praises forever. Spread your protection over them, that all who love your name may be filled with joy. For you bless the godly, O LORD; you surround them with your shield of love. (Psalm 5:11-12)
- You will keep in perfect peace all who trust in you, all whose thoughts are fixed on you! Trust in the LORD always, for the LORD GOD is the eternal Rock. (Isaiah 26:3-4)

Write the scripture that you chose in your journal. Meditate on this verse throughout the day and remind yourself that all things are possible to them who believe.

## Time in His Presence

Spend some time with God meditating on your transformation scripture. What do you think the Lord is speaking to you through this verse?

## Life Application

Ask Holy Spirit to help you apply this scripture to your daily life. How can I apply this to my life today?

## Prayer

If you acknowledge that God is faithful and that He can always be trusted, then please pray with me:

*Lord, thank You for being good, faithful, kind, and trustworthy. I choose to trust You today in the midst of the circumstances. No matter what I face in this life, I know that You are always good, and that You can always be trusted. My faith in You is a shield that surrounds my life with Your favor and goodness. Help me to trust You always, and to take steps of faith as You lead me. Thank you, Lord! In Jesus' name I pray. Amen."*

# Chapter 8

# A Life of Purpose

## Keys to Lifestyle Management

*And [I pray] that the eyes of your heart [the very center and core of your being] may be enlightened [flooded with light by the Holy Spirit], so that you will know and cherish the hope [the divine guarantee, the confident expectation] to which He has called you, the riches of His glorious inheritance in the saints (God's people), and [so that you will begin to know] what the immeasurable and unlimited and surpassing greatness of His [active, spiritual] power is in us who believe. These are in accordance with the working of His mighty strength which He produced in Christ when He raised Him from the dead and seated Him at His own right hand in the heavenly places.*
—Ephesians 1:18-20 AMP

As you are consistently pursuing God each day, and being faithful in the small things, your life becomes supernaturally productive. I remember seeing this in my own life. My relationship with God fueled me from the inside out, and literally caused me to be unstoppable in my pursuit of life. I wasn't stalking success, but success found me—in everything that I put my hand to because I was prioritizing my relationship with God above all else. It was as if God was so blessed by our time together that He pursued ways to bless me in return. This became a constant, joyful exchange between a Daddy and His daughter, as I discovered Him and His desire to spend time with me.

I looked forward to getting up in the morning, and running to the secret place with Him. During that time, God would speak to me, fill me with vision for my future, and give me ideas that would shape my life and my character for His glory. My simple habit of reading the Bible every day led me to get up even earlier in the morning so that I could spend more time with God, which led to a complete life transformation. I became so encouraged by the fruit from this small habit, that I decided to implement healthy habits in every area of my life. This one small decision charged my life with energy and passion, which fueled me to fulfill my life's purpose!

How did this happen? It came from a relationship with the Creator. When we spend time with the One who created us, we understand that we were created for a purpose. God is a god of vision. He sees perfectly His plan for the world He created and each person within it. Not everyone is fulfilling God's purpose for their life because they lack a relationship with the One who created them. Everyone's purpose is to be in a relationship with God. From that intimate relationship, we discover our true selves, God's original plan for our life.

When you begin to live from this relationship with the Creator, each day you are living from and for Him, and your life is filled with purpose that is far greater than you could ever dream to ask for. This purpose comes from God alone, and it is the only place in life where you find true fulfillment and satisfaction. In your relationship with God, you not only find your purpose, but you discover that He has equipped you with the tools you need to fulfill it.

Throughout this chapter, I am going to highlight some simple principles from the Word of God that will help you manage your life in a godly way, so that you can pursue your purpose with success. These are some of the principles that God has taught me through time with Him, with His Word, and from the teachers in my life. These principles will cause untold blessings to overflow into every area of your life—just like they did in mine. Because they come from God's Word, they ensure consistent positive results to all those who follow them.

## The Power of Preparation

In the Bible, you see many parables about what the kingdom is like. The parable of the ten virgins and their lanterns is a parable about being prepared. Matthew 25:1-13 (NKJV) says,

> Then the kingdom of heaven shall be likened to ten virgins who took their lamps and went out to meet the bridegroom. Now five of them were wise, and five were foolish. Those who were foolish took their lamps and took no oil with them, but the wise took oil in their vessels with their lamps. But while the bridegroom was delayed, they all slumbered and slept. And at midnight a cry was heard: "Behold, the bridegroom is coming; go out to meet him!" Then all those virgins arose and trimmed their lamps. And the foolish said to the wise, "Give us some of your oil, for our lamps are going out." But the wise answered, saying, "No, lest there should not be enough for us

and you; but go rather to those who sell, and buy for yourselves." And while they went to buy, the bridegroom came, and those who were ready went in with him to the wedding; and the door was shut. Afterward the other virgins came also, saying, "Lord, Lord, open to us!" But he answered and said, "Assuredly, I say to you, I do not know you. Watch therefore, for you know neither the day nor the hour in which the Son of Man is coming.

I appreciate the parables that Jesus told because they give us insight to the kingdom of heaven. In this parable, all of the virgins were there to see the Lord, but five were wise and five were foolish (vv 1-2). What makes someone wise and another person a fool? Well, the Bible says, "The fear of the LORD is the beginning of wisdom, and the knowledge of the Holy One is understanding" (Prov. 9:10 NKJV). The Bible also says, "Fools think their own way is right, but the wise listen to others" (Prov. 12:15). This tells you that reverence for God, His will, and His ways counts you as wise. Rejecting God and His counsel because you think you're right makes you a fool. When God gives you counsel from His Word, leads you by His Spirit, or gives you correction, it is not to hurt you. God leads you because He loves you, and He is trying to prepare you for what's to come: Jesus! Get ready, get prepared, and be wise. Don't be a fool and reject His instruction of preparation.

How do you get prepared for Jesus? Use the life you've been given, and don't waste it. The Virtuous Woman in the Bible feared God, worked hard, held herself accountable, and showed up for life every day. Please take a moment to read this passage in Proverbs 31:10-31. The Virtuous Woman had a reverent relationship with God, and from that relationship she gained spiritual strength that fueled her life with power and purpose. As a result, she was a bright light that gave life back to others. Her life impacted God, herself, her family, the poor, and the people of the city. Everything she set her hands to prospered, and everything she touched was blessed. Those who reverence God are those who yield to His instruction. When you do this, you are laying your life down and saying, "God, You are Lord of my life. I trust that Your ways are better than mine, so I yield my actions as an act of submission to You. I will do the things that You're leading me to do by Your ability, not my own." The person who lives their life this way every day will be productive, fruitful, and prepared for Jesus' coming.

This life is not your own. You are not here for yourself. You are here for God, to bear fruit for Him, to take the gospel to the ends of the earth, and to fulfill His calling for your life. God has a purpose for you that is far greater than you can imagine. Spend your time on the earth accomplishing God's will so you will be ready when Christ returns.

## The Power of Vision

Proverbs 29:18 (KJV) says, "Where there is no vision, the people perish: but he that keepeth the law, happy is he." [1]The word *vision* in Hebrew means mental sight, a dream, or revelation. Especially a vision from God respecting future events. If you do not have a dream from God about your future, a positive expectation about what's coming, then you are headed for destruction. You need to have a plan for your life, and it needs to come from God!

When you receive vision from God about your future, you can journal it, speak it, and create a vision board. A vision board is a visual collection of images that represent your dreams, and it will help take your dreams from the inside of you, to in front of you, to manifesting it in your life. It shows you the possibilities for your future, helps change the image on the inside of you, and produces hope and motivation within you to bring them forth. Habakkuk 2:2-3 (NASB) says, "Then the LORD answered me and said, "Write down the vision and inscribe it clearly on tablets, so that one who reads it may run. "For the vision is yet for the appointed time; it hurries toward the goal and it will not fail. Though it delays, wait for it; for it will certainly come, it will not delay long." Get the vision that God has placed within you on the outside of you through writing it down, and making it plain. Imagine this vision for your future coming to pass in your life, and see yourself living and experiencing your dreams.

Terri Savelle Foy is a best-selling author, founder of an international ministry and a success coach to people around the world. Her encouraging teaching has inspired me to keep pursuing my dreams a countless number of times. [2]In her book, *Imagine Big*, she says,

> *When what you see in your imagination is bigger than what you see in your reality, you will begin to attract the ideas, opportunities, resources, faith and relationships necessary to pursue those dreams.*
> – Terri Savelle Foy

Have you ever heard of the Law of Attraction? This principle states that you will attract to your life the things that you focus on. You will receive what you believe. [3]Even though this philosophy was named in the early 1900s, it first originated in the Bible. Proverbs 23:7 says, "For as he thinks in his heart, so is he." Your vision and imagination are powerful tools that can bring transformation to your life! The goal is to transform the way you see your life on the inside, so that it will manifest on the outside.

God created you perfectly, and He sees you perfectly. He created you with unlimited potential. Sometimes, you can be the worst judge of yourself, and your hardest critic. In order to walk in God's purpose for your life, you must agree with Him, and the way He sees you! Believe that He loves you and wants your life to abound with all good things. When you can believe this, imagine it, and see it in your heart, then you will bring forth the things you're hoping for.

> **In order to walk in God's purpose for your life, you must begin to agree with Him, and the way He sees you!**

Now faith is the substance of things hoped for, the evidence of things not seen. (Hebrews 11:1 NKJV)

God has given you many tools to help you live a successful, prospering life. He has even equipped you with the same abilities that He has: His heart, His mind, His Spirit, His faith, and His Name. God created you in His image, and He has given you the same ability to create that He has! Well, God had to see the earth before He spoke it into existence. In order to bring forth the dreams inside of you, you need to do the same things He did. Believe the dreams inside of you are from God, see them by getting your vision in front of you, and speak them forth through positive declarations! To help you get started on your vision board, I have created an entire chapter in my *Walking in the New You! Workbook* specifically to elaborate on this topic. Chapter 5 in my workbook deals entirely with vision, helping you to dream big with God and to create a vision board for your life.

# The Power of a Plan

Once you receive vision regarding God's purpose for your life, create a plan for how you're going to accomplish it.

> Through wisdom a house is built, and by understanding it is established; By knowledge the rooms are filled with all precious and pleasant riches.
>
> A wise man is strong, yes, a man of knowledge increases strength; For by wise counsel you will wage your own war, and in a multitude of counselors there is safety. (Proverbs 24:3-6)

These verses tell you that there is power in a plan. You can't just throw a house together. A house is built through wisdom, preparation, and understanding. After it's built, the house becomes full of precious treasures and pleasant riches through knowledge. The scriptures go on to tell you that the same wisdom and planning it takes to build a house is the same wisdom and planning required to make a man strong, to wage a war, and to prepare your future.

This type of wise planning creates security for your future physically, naturally, financially, and spiritually. My *Walking in the New You! Workbook* and *Productivity Planner* are full of tools and trackers to help you take control of your future! These resources discuss biblical principles that you can apply to every area of your life: spirit, soul, body, health, finances, relationships, home, fitness, and nutrition.

## The Power of a Routine

Finally, how can you ensure that you will see success in your life and see your purpose come to pass?

For me, if there is something that the Lord has told me to implement in my life, then I make it a habit by setting up routines, or disciplines for each area of my life. Routines and habits ensure that I make time for the things that empower my spirit instead of my flesh, which I discuss more in Chapter 11 of this book. In order for me to maintain consistency in my life, I have created specific time slots so that I can accomplish the desires in my heart.

Early in my sobriety, God showed me areas of my life that He wanted to heal through healthy habits and routines. The first thing He revealed to me was His Word. I started by reading one verse a day every morning. I became so blessed by the fruit this produced that I decided to start another routine. Over time, people began to see changes in my life, and my habits began to impact other people. This simple practice has revolutionized my life and it has impacted the lives around me. In fact, God is able to trust me in this area so much that He's opened the door for me to write a book about it and create a ministry around it! Who knew that being faithful in these little things could transform a broken life and turn it into something beautiful?

> **Routines and habits ensure that I make time for the things that empower my spirit instead of my flesh.**

Most of my routines are daily habits, but some of them are weekly. For example, I set aside time to call my parents every week, and my grandparents on Fridays. I plan our meals on Wednesday night, pick up groceries on Thursday night, and cook on Friday night. Then, my husband and I clean the house on Friday night, so that we can enjoy the remainder of the weekend. Here are a handful of my favorite routines that have really stuck with me:

Daily:

- Get up early
- Praise God
- Be thankful
- Read the Bible
- Journal
- Pray
- Positive confessions
- Drink water
- Exercise
- Write my book
- Work towards a goal
- Eat healthy
- Drink a fruit-and-veggie smoothie
- Pick up messes around the house, and wipe down counters

Weekly:

- Time with family
- Time with friends
- Call relatives
- Clean
- Spend time outside
- Healthy nutrition: meal prep
- Be active

Just because these are the things that work for me doesn't mean that these are the best options for you and your family. Hopefully, this can give you some ideas for your life.

Over time, small habits revolutionized my life. They helped me save money, get healthier, and ultimately led me to my destiny and purpose. Don't despise small beginnings, and don't despise the small desires in your heart. They may be leading you to your purpose!

> **Don't despise small beginnings, and don't despise the small desires in your heart.**

When you create a routine in your life, you are propelling yourself towards success. This is an atmosphere of order, faithfulness, consistency, and diligence. Another word you could use for this is intentionality. A lifestyle of intentionality will always produce increase in your life. This type of intentional living produces endurance for your soul and body, and it creates a lifestyle of empowerment from the inside out. This is inside-out living, or living from your spirit, which fuels your soul and strengthens your body.

# Managing Your Time

The morning time is my favorite time to accomplish my routines because no one else is awake, and no one needs me at 4 a.m. in the morning. Also, by the time I get home from work, I'm tired, and it's harder for me to fellowship with God, write, and exercise after a busy day of work. The Bible also tells you to give God your first fruits: the first fruit is talking about your finances, the first 10% of your income. But, I also like to give God the first of my day, and the first of my week at church. Of course, I try to communicate with God all day long, and meditate on the Word and ask Him for help. But it is essential for the believer to have one-on-one time with God where you can read the Word, pray, and listen to His voice.

To give you an example of how I manage my time, here is what an average weekday looks like for me:

- 4:00 a.m. Wake up, let the dog out, make coffee.
- 4:15–5:00 a.m. Quiet time with God.
- 5:00–5:45 a.m. Write my book or work towards my goals.
- 5:45–6:30 a.m. Cardio and strength training.
- 6:30–6:45 a.m. Read the Bible and pray with my husband.
- 6:45–7:45 a.m. Get ready for work.
- 8:00 a.m.–4:30 p.m. Work.
- 5:00–6:00 p.m. Dinner at home.
- 6:00–7:30 p.m. Free time.
- 7:30 p.m. Get ready for bed and read.
- 8:00 p.m. Sleep.

Evaluate how you spend your time. Remember, I did not start here. I grew to the place where I cherished my mornings with God, and the fruit that came from this. The fruit of daily good decisions caused me to value my time tremendously. Ten minutes a day, five days a week, can change your life just like it did mine. Find the time that works for you where you can create healthy habits and turn them into a routine. My *Walking in the New You! Workbook* has a special section on Time Management to help you gain control of your time and plan success into your day!

> The fruit of daily good decisions caused me to value my time tremendously.

## A Habit Becomes a Lifestyle

If you remain consistent and faithful to these commitments, they will become a lifestyle. I have found that remaining true to myself helps me to remain true to God and true to others. When I make time to accomplish the desires that God has placed in my heart, I can show up for my family, friends, and co-workers, filled up and full of life because I took care of my relationship with God first—the Life Source. You are just as important as the people around you! You deserve to be faithful to yourself, and consistent to achieving the desires in your heart.

The very first commandment from God is, "You shall have no other gods before Me" (Exodus 20:3). That means that God needs to be first in your life. Anything that comes before your relationship with God is an idol in your life, and you have created another god. Love Him first, with everything within you, and make time for Him. After you give to God first, He will strengthen you to accomplish the commitments you've made to yourself, and also to others.

> **After you give to God first, He will strengthen you to accomplish the commitments you've made to yourself, and also to others.**

Even if mornings aren't your favorite, I encourage you to be open-minded to the possibility of becoming a morning person. I used to despise getting up early, exercising, and being healthy, but I changed. I declare over myself out loud, "I love the morning time. I love to read the Word and spend time with God. I love to work out, eat healthy, be healthy, and think healthy." I learned to enjoy things that were good for me. They added vibrancy and prosperity to every area of my life.

It's the life and heart of God for you to live an active, strong, prospering life in your spirit, soul, and body. It all starts from the spirit man, your relationship with God, His Word, and His Spirit. If you are moving towards accomplishing your purpose for the Lord, all of those declarations that I mentioned will benefit your life. If you can implement each of those things into your life as a habit, you will move towards a productive and purposeful life with God.

The time that you set aside to be with God, and accomplish your dreams, will become your strength in life; your refuge where you can run to God, seek His wisdom, and receive shelter from the storm. When you honor God and give Him part of your life and part of every day, you will receive supernatural strength and endurance to achieve the desires in your heart.

> Blessed [fortunate, prosperous, and favored by God] is the man who does not walk in the counsel of the wicked [following their advice and example], nor stand in the path of sinners, nor sit [down to rest] in the seat of scoffers (ridiculers). But his delight is in the law of the LORD, and on His law [His precepts and teachings] he [habitually] meditates day and

night. And he will be like a tree *firmly* planted [and fed] by streams of water, which yields its fruit in its season; its leaf does not wither; and in whatever he does, he prospers [and comes to maturity].
(Psalm 1:1-3 AMP)

Ask God to give you a next step for your life. Then, ask Him to help you accomplish it every day. He will not force you! But, if you set aside time, He will bless the time you give Him, and help you achieve it.

Start with one new routine in your life and ask God to highlight the most important area for *you* during this time. You have been called for such a time as this (Esther 4:14). This time in your life is essential. Redeem the time that you've been given (Ephesians 5:16), and make the most of it. Barry Bennett is a wise and beloved teacher at the Bible College I attended, Charis Bible College. He says, "You will make time for what matters most to you." If God is important to you, then you will make time for Him in your life. If you really want to see changes in your life, then make time for what truly matters. The desires in your heart will not magically come to pass. It requires faith, relationship with God, and dedication to His Word and ways.

Visualize your purpose, and dreams, and speak them forth with faith! I recommend reviewing your vision and dreams consistently. As you make progress, and take steps of faith, you will be amazed to see how God is working on your side! The momentum of good, proactive decisions will cause your dreams to be closer and closer each day. Taking small steps each day will cause you to make huge leaps towards your purpose! Before you know it, you will be living the life of your dreams!

# Transform Your Life

## Application of Chapter Concepts

### A Moment of Reflection: Saying "Yes" To God's Proposal

1. How does it make you feel to know that God wants to partner with you to bring success to your life?

2. Do you have a vision or direction for your future?
    - How can you prepare for the purpose God's given you?
        1. Create a plan for how you can start taking small steps to accomplish that purpose. Is there a next step God is leading you to take?
        2. How can you create a routine to ensure consistency in that next step?

3. How can you manage your time more efficiently, if at all?

4. Spend time alone with God, and let Him guide your heart. What is the next step of faith that you can take in these areas? What do you sense He is leading you to do next? Listen to His voice, and write down thoughts that come to your mind. Remember, God's voice will always agree with the Word. If a thought comes that contradicts God's Word, you can replace it with the truth.

## My Transformation Scripture

What is a scripture that speaks to you about the power of a life of purpose? Here are a few suggestions:

- Who saved us and called us to a holy calling, not because of our works but because of his own purpose and grace, which he gave us in Christ Jesus before the ages began. (2 Timothy 1:9 ESV)
- "For I know the plans I have for you," says the LORD. "They are plans for good and not for disaster, to give you a future and a hope. (Jeremiah 29:11)
- Furthermore, because we are united with Christ, we have received an inheritance from God, for he chose us in advance, and he makes everything work out according to his plan. (Ephesians 1:11)
- Then the way you live will always honor and please the Lord, and your lives will produce every kind of

good fruit. All the while, you will grow as you learn to know God better and better. (Colossians 1:10)
- But before they were born, before they had done anything good or bad, she received a message from God. (This message shows that God chooses people according to his own purposes.) (Romans 9:11)
- And [I pray] that the eyes of your heart [the very center and core of your being] may be enlightened [flooded with light by the Holy Spirit], so that you will know and cherish the hope [the divine guarantee, the confident expectation] to which He has called you, the riches of His glorious inheritance in the saints (God's people), and [so that you will begin to know] what the immeasurable and unlimited and surpassing greatness of His [active, spiritual] power is in us who believe. These are in accordance with the working of His mighty strength. (Ephesians 1:18-19 AMP)

Write the scripture that you chose in your journal. Meditate on this verse throughout the day and remind yourself of God's purpose for your life.

## Time in His Presence

Spend some time with God meditating on your transformation scripture. What do you think the Lord is speaking to you through this verse?

## Life Application

Ask Holy Spirit to help you apply this scripture to your daily life. How can I apply this to my life today?

## Prayer

If you are ready to live a life of purpose, and pursue the dreams that God has placed within you, then please pray with me:

*Lord, thank You for proposing a life of purpose to me. I say, "Yes!" I want every good thing that You have for me, and I will lay down my life so that I can walk in Your will. Make it clear to me how You are leading me. Help me rely on Your strength to prepare my life for Your purpose. Show me how to manage my time well, so I can be consistent with healthy habits. In Jesus's name I pray. Amen.*

# Chapter 9

# The Power of Daily Commitment

## Consistency Will Always Produce Success!

*The master was full of praise. "Well done, my good and faithful servant. You have been faithful in handling this small amount, so now I will give you many more responsibilities. Let's celebrate together!"*
—Matthew 25:21

Ever since I decided to live my life for God, I have had many, many, many opportunities to give up. In fact, just yesterday I was faced with an issue that was followed by the thought, *Should I just stop here and give up?* Well, praise God that we have the Holy Spirit within us who strengthens us and gives us grace to keep working towards the goal. I want to finish my race and stand before God knowing that I gave Him every ounce of strength that I had in this lifetime!

In this life, you will face battles, persecutions, and sufferings that will try to take you out, cause you to quit, or make you want to give up. Paul says that he rejoices in these sufferings.

> We can rejoice, too, when we run into problems and trials, for we know that they help us develop endurance. And endurance develops strength of character, and character strengthens our confident hope of salvation. And this hope will not lead to disappointment. For we know how dearly God loves us, because he has given us the Holy Spirit to fill our hearts with his love. (Romans 5:3-5)

For many of us, rejoicing in our suffering is an entirely new concept. But if the Bible says it, we can believe it and we can do it! When we face problems, trials, and tribulations with a positive, godly attitude, we will see the victory. God promises victory to His children. We just need to remain faithful, consistent, and exercise endurance in the midst of the trial.

Many years ago, I faced a battle and I wanted to run away, leave the situation, and give up. My mentor advised me, "When David faced Goliath in the Bible, he didn't run from him, he ran towards him. Because David chose to face his giant, he defeated him, and received the victory. That victory included freedom for the nation of Israel, and it promoted David giving him entrance into the king's court. Consider this situation as your Goliath. Are you going to run towards your giant or away from it? If you run from it, then you will have to face it again until you defeat it."

Every day, you are presented with choices. What to wear, what to eat, what to drink, what to do, what to say, and the list could go on forever. God has given you so many tools and resources to equip your life for success. You don't have to be victorious one day, and down in the dumps the next day.

> **Great success does not come from one great decision. Long-term success is the result of several small decisions over a length of time.**

You can run towards your giants and face them without fear knowing that the God of Israel is on your side. Because you are a child of God, you carry the covenant anointing to remain in victory no matter what your circumstances may say. This means that whatever comes against you, your place of sonship will carry you through.

Great success does not come from one great decision. Long-term success is the result of several small decisions over a length of time. Those small decisions to show up every day and face the battle with love and gentleness will lead to endurance, strength of character, and hope. A daily commitment to God in every area of your life will ensure that your soul stands the test of time when the battle gets rough.

# Faithfulness

No matter what, show up every day! Be faithful in everything you do. This will go a long way and take you very far in life.

In Matthew 25:14-30, Jesus tells a parable of the talents. This is a story of a man who travels into a far country and leaves his possessions with three servants. One servant received five talents, another received two, and the last received one. Both the servant who received five talents, and the servant who received two talents, went and invested their master's possessions so that they gained more from it. The servant that received one talent was afraid, and he dug his master's possessions in the ground. When the master returned, he said this to the servants who gained him more, 'Well done, good and faithful servant; you were faithful over a few things, I will make you ruler over many things. Enter into the joy of your lord' (Matthew 25:21). To the other servant he said, "You wicked and lazy servant, you knew that I reap where I have not sown, and gather where I have not scattered seed. So you ought to have deposited my money with the bankers, and at my coming I would have received back my own with interest. So take the talent from him, and give it to him who has ten talents. 'For to everyone who has, more will be given, and he will have abundance; but from him who does not have, even what he has will be taken away. And cast the unprofitable servant into the outer darkness. There will be weeping and gnashing of teeth'" (Matt. 25:26-30 NKJV).

There is so much that you could glean from this parable, but one thing is, don't be intimidated and hide what God has given you. Instead, use your life and the talents that God has given you and sow them by faith! When you step out in faith, you are giving God something to work with! When you don't do anything, you will remain right where you are, and no one is getting blessed by the ability God has given you.

Everyone has something. If you can see, use your eyesight to bless God and other people. If you can walk, use your strength for God and bless someone else. Your life can be used to bless other people right where you are! Every day, you can show up and be faithful right where you are. Don't wait for God to drop your purpose in your lap. Your purpose is right in front of you: serving the people around you with love, hard work, integrity, and honor.

If you are sitting around waiting for something to change in your life, then God is going to say, "You wicked and lazy servant!" Don't wait for your life to change before you decide to change. Change your life! When you show up for life faithfully with a smile on your face and a positive attitude, you are using what God has given you. He will say, "Well done, good and faithful servant!" And *then* He will give you more responsibility.

# Consistency Produces Confidence

God is the best example of consistency that you have. When God says something, He does it. God is so reliable and consistent that the Bible says, He is the same throughout all time. "Jesus Christ is the same yesterday, today, and forever" (Heb. 13:8).

Titus 2:7 says, "And you yourself must be an example to them by doing good works of every kind. Let everything you do reflect the integrity and seriousness of your teaching." This verse tells you that in all things, in everything you do, show yourself to be a pattern of good works. That means at home, at work, in your relationship with God, in the marketplace, everywhere you go, in everything you say, in everything you do you are representing God. In all things you can choose to bear the fruit of godliness and good works. Why is this important? If you read on in Titus 2, he tells you:

Not pilfering, but showing all good faith, so that in everything they may adorn the doctrine of God our Savior. For the grace of God has appeared, bringing salvation for all people, training us to renounce ungodliness and worldly passions, and to live self-controlled, upright, and godly lives in the present age, waiting for our blessed hope, the appearing of the glory of our great God and Savior Jesus Christ, who gave himself for us to redeem us from all lawlessness and to purify for himself a people for his own possession who are zealous for good works. Declare these things; exhort and rebuke with all authority. Let no one disregard you.
(Titus 2:10-15 ESV)

When you consistently model your life after God and the instruction in His Word, you are adorning the doctrine of God in all things! That means that you are causing God's Word to look beautiful upon you, upon your life, your actions; and you are glorifying God, and making Him look good. That is so awesome! The promises of God manifest in your life are a direct result of you honoring God's Word by doing God's Word, and your life bears the fruit of His goodness! You will see healing, prosperity, deliverance, freedom, and salvation spring forth in every area of your life, and it's beautiful! It's beautiful to God, to you, and to those around you. You are adorning your life with the goodness of God! And notice it's not by your might and ability, but by the grace and ability of God within you (vv 11). The same grace that has appeared to all men to save them, is the same grace that God has given to equip you with the ability to deny ungodliness and live according to godliness *in this present age.* Because, there is hope for those who live this way. Jesus Christ is coming back for His bride, the church. He wants us to be ready for Him when He comes back! Life on earth is preparation time. Every day, the Spirit of God is quickening His wisdom to you, leading you and guiding you to prepare yourself for His return.

To help you prepare for Christ's return, be consistent! Consistency is a key to succeeding in life. You honor God, yourself, and others when you are consistent in keeping your commitments. To help you keep your commitments to others, be sure that you keep your commitments to yourself. If you decide you want to start a new routine, then make time for it, and rely on God to help you keep that commitment to yourself. That's what God's grace is for! God's grace is His strength *through your weaknesses* (2 Cor. 12:9-10). When it comes time to do it, ask God to help you, and don't allow your flesh and emotions to talk you out of it. Give yourself permission to be consistent. Show up for yourself and keep that commitment. You are worth it. You can accomplish what you set your mind and heart to with God. You honor God when you honor your word, and you will be someone that God, and others, can depend on.

Consistency will produce confidence in your life. When you continually show up for life and honor your word, you will grow in confidence because you're able to trust yourself. When you can trust yourself and the things you say, then it provides stability within your heart. You will not look for value outside of your relationship with God because God is what gives your life value. When you consistently do what God is leading you to do, you will not be condemned when people persecute you, or judge you. Being right with God is the only thing that matters in life. When you are right with God, everything else will fall into place.

---

**Consistency will produce confidence in your life.**

---

Therefore, my beloved brethren, be steadfast, immovable, always abounding in the work of the Lord, knowing that your labor is not in vain in the Lord. (1 Corinthians 15:58)

When you apply the Word of God correctly to your life, it will help you to imitate God from your spirit, through your soul, and into your body. The blessings of living a godly life every day will be a constant flow of life to you and through you to the people around you. Small steps of trusting faithfulness will produce a life of consistent success.

If you are trying to get somewhere on a map, then you can't drive a straight line. You have to follow directions, make turns, yield to other drivers, and sometimes even turn around. If you notice that you've been following the wrong map in life, that's ok! God is not mad at you. Just repent, and change the direction you're going. Start following God with all of your heart, and make your actions align with God's will. Make choices today that will help you accomplish who you want to be tomorrow.

Success in life comes from one decision, one moment at a time, throughout a lifetime. Faith and patience inherit the promises. You need to exercise faith every day over a prolonged period of time in order to see the fruit of

God's promises fulfilled in your life. Don't give up. See things through eyes of faith and the truth written in God's Word. Over time, your daily commitment to God will bring you success, restoration, and transformation to every area of your life.

# Transform Your Life
## Application of Chapter Concepts

### A Moment of Reflection: Making Time Today for Tomorrow's Transformation

1. Is there an area of your life where you've been tempted to quit, give up, and not show up? How is God leading you in that area of your life?

2. What are some areas of your life where you would like to practice faithfulness and consistency?

    - If you could be consistent in those areas for an entire year, how do you think it could transform your life this year?
    - If you can be consistent in those areas for five years, how would it transform your life? (Consistency in these areas today will lead to tomorrow's transformation!)

3. Spend time alone with God, and let Him guide your heart. What is the next step of faith that you can take in these areas? What do you sense He is leading you

to do next? Listen to His voice, and write down thoughts that come to your mind. Remember, God's voice will always agree with the Word. If a thought comes that contradicts God's Word, you can replace it with the truth.

## My Transformation Scripture

What is a scripture that speaks to you about the power of a daily commitment to God's Word and being faithful in the small things? Here are a few suggestions:

- Seek the Kingdom of God above all else, and live righteously, and he will give you everything you need. (Matthew 6:33)
- For assuredly, I say to you, whoever says to this mountain, "Be removed and be cast into the sea," and does not doubt in his heart, but believes that those things he says will be done, he will have whatever he says. (Mark 11:23 NKJV)
- And the seed that fell on good soil represents those who hear and accept God's word and produce a harvest of thirty, sixty, or even a hundred times as much as had been planted! (Mark 4:20)

- If you are faithful in little things, you will be faithful in large ones. But if you are dishonest in little things, you won't be honest with greater responsibilities. (Luke 16:10)
- And whatever you do or say, do it as a representative of the Lord Jesus, giving thanks through him to God the Father. (Colossians 3:17)
- So, my dear brothers and sisters, be strong and immovable. Always work enthusiastically for the Lord, for you know that nothing you do for the Lord is ever useless. (1 Corinthians 15:58)

Write the scripture that you chose in your journal. Meditate on this verse throughout the day, and remind yourself of the power of a daily commitment to the things of God.

### Time in His Presence

Spend some time with God meditating on your transformation scripture. What do you think the Lord is speaking to you through this verse?

## Life Application

Ask Holy Spirit to help you apply this scripture to your daily life. How can I apply this to my life today?

## Prayer

If you are ready to apply God's Word to your life and make a daily commitment to living your life for Him, then please pray with me:

*Lord, thank You for filling my life with power and ability through my relationship with You. Thank You for giving me Your Word to live by, and to guide my life to victory and purpose. I ask Holy Spirit to help me every day to live my life for You, from Your strength and ability. Help me to be faithful and consistent in everything that You tell me to do, Lord. In Jesus' name I pray. Amen.*

# Chapter 10

## Strong in Faith

### Living in Freedom Every Day

*But he did not doubt or waver in unbelief concerning the promise of God, but he grew strong and empowered by faith, giving glory to God.*
—Romans 4:20 AMP

The world tries to tempt you with quick fixes, sensual pleasures, or get-rich-quick schemes that only leave you feeling empty and hopeless. When you say "yes" to the world's version of "fixes," it only leads to more bondage and captivity. You feel like you're trapped in a cycle that never gives you what it offers you, and it depletes your energy and your resources as you try to crawl out of the hole it dug for you. I'm all too familiar with these things. Gladly, I am now more familiar with the freedom of living life with God. The still, small voice of God that can only be caught by being sought, provides you with freedom unlike anything this world can offer you. God's freedom fills you with inner peace, joy, contentment, and love that fuels your life with passion. God's freedom causes you to want to get out of bed in the morning and pursue life, instead of snoozing your alarm five times and dreading the day ahead.

Trust me, I have lived both lives, and God's way is the best way. This type of life is supernatural and demands an explanation that human words can't justify. Through faith in Jesus Christ, I have discovered a life full of freedom, satisfaction, and contentment that endures the test of time. And it just keeps getting better because God continues to teach me *how to use my faith*. Faith is essential to walking in God's freedom. To access the fullness of that freedom, we must learn to cooperate with the spiritual principles of faith that God has set in place. There are simple things that we can do each day to help us strengthen our faith, and use our faith with power behind it.

Hebrews 11:1 (NKJV) says, "Now faith is the *substance of things hoped for,* the evidence of things not seen." Your faith is spiritual substance for whatever you're hoping for! It has the ability to bring the unseen realm into the seen realm; to bring what is in the spirit into the natural. Your faith helps you resist the world's temptations so you can walk in complete freedom. Only from this place of faith-filled-freedom will you be able to finish your race with strength, endure hardness, and not grow weary in well doing. Being strong in faith is essential for walking out the Christian life in victory. Who's ready to strengthen their faith? Let's get started!

## The Grace and Faith of Christ

Every promise that you receive in the Christian life is by the grace of God through your faith. Some people may read this and think that they need more faith. Did you know that God has given every person an equal measure of faith (Rom. 12:3)? In the book of Galatians, it says that God has given you **His faith,** and it is by His faith that you are justified (Gal. 2:16, 20). When you receive Jesus Christ as your Lord and Savior, He gives you His faith and now His faith becomes your faith. This should take a lot of pressure off of you! You don't need to pray and ask for more faith, you just need to learn how to use the faith that God has given you.

> For by grace you have been saved through faith. And this is not your own doing; it is the gift of God, not a result of works, so that no one may boast. For we are his workmanship, created in Christ Jesus for good works, which God prepared beforehand, that we should walk in them. (Ephesians 2:8-10 ESV)

The grace of God has forgiven you, saved you, given you faith, and causes you to enter into all of the promises of God in Christ Jesus. [1]In the Bible, *grace* is the Greek word *charis,* which is translated to mean the divine influence upon the heart, and its reflection in life; including gratitude, benefit, favor, gift, joy, liberality, and pleasure. The grace of God is His divine help, ability, influence, and provision in your life. You access all the blessings of God and move forward through the entire Christian life by God's grace through faith. The moment you try to start doing things by works, and not by faith, you have left God's grace. Staying in God's grace is essential!

> **You access all the blessings of God and move forward through the entire Christian life by God's grace through faith.**

Every day, I have to remind myself to use my faith in order to stay in God's grace. It is a constant temptation for me to try to start performing in order to receive what I'm believing for. For example, when God told me it was time to write this book. I said, "Okay, let's do this, God!" I knew that only with God's help would I be able to accomplish His calling on my life.

Starting out, I was strong in faith. I began by getting up early and writing a little bit every morning. A few months in, I hit some obstacles along the way. Writing this book was taking longer than I expected, and my words on the page weren't forming as clearly as I wanted them to. My eyes and my heart moved off of God and His ability (grace), and I began to focus on myself and my inability. This caused me to get discouraged and emotional. I became frustrated because I was completely out of faith, only looking at it from my perspective and limited ability.

Has there been a situation in your life where you stepped out of God's grace, and relied on yourself? Did you experience a similar frustration? Well, I'm happy to say that it's a simple, internal shift to get back into grace.

Anytime that our focus shifts off of God and onto our performance or ability, we have moved out of God's grace. Frustration, discouragement, fear, anxiety, and doubt are some of the indicators that we are depending on ourselves instead of relying on God's grace to get the job done. So, how do we get back into God's grace, ability, strength, and provision? By faith! As soon as we recognize that we are operating outside of God's grace, we can simply acknowledge, "God, I can't do anything without you. Can you please help me?" This simple surrender and internal shift will move us into our powerful place of trusting God by faith, and relying on His grace to carry us through. To accomplish our calling in the Christian life, we must rely on God's grace through faith. Without God, I can do nothing (John 15:5), but with God nothing will be impossible (Luke 1:37).

---

**To accomplish our calling in the Christian life, we must rely on God's grace through faith.**

# Praying in Tongues

One way that you can strengthen your faith is by praying in tongues. Maybe this is a new concept for you, or maybe it isn't. I encourage you to have an open mind and try praying in tongues before you write it off completely. For me, my life transformed when I began to pray in tongues consistently. It strengthens my inner man of faith, gives me wisdom from God, encourages me, fills me with the love of God, and builds me up on my most holy faith.

Praying in tongues is for every born-again believer. In fact, Jesus said that it would be a sign that you believe in Him (Mark 16:17). In the New Testament church, those who believed were then baptized in the Holy Spirit and they spoke with tongues (Acts 2:3-4, 10:44-46, 19:6). The Apostle Paul wrote most of the books and epistles in the New Testament of the Bible and he said that he prayed in tongues more than anyone (1 Cor. 14:18). He trusted that it was a powerful gift from God, and as a result, it filled his life with spiritual wisdom, revelation, and power. There are many other verses in the Bible about the benefits of praying in tongues. Such as, you will speak mysteries (1 Cor. 14:2), edify yourself (1 Cor. 14:4), your spirit is praying (1 Cor.

14:14), you are drawing on the wisdom of God (1 Cor. 2:10-13), and the Spirit of God is praying on your behalf (Rom. 8:26).

The Bible says in Jude 1:20-21 (NKJV), "But you, beloved, building yourselves up on your most holy faith, praying in the Holy Spirit, keep yourselves in the love of God, looking for the mercy of our Lord Jesus Christ unto eternal life." When you pray in tongues you are building up yourself on your most holy faith, keeping yourself in the love of God. ²*Looking for* in Greek means to admit (to intercourse, hospitality, credence, or endurance); to await with confidence or patience; accept, allow, look and wait for, take. When you pray in tongues you are having intimate fellowship with God, receiving endurance, confidence, patience, and allowing all of the goodness of God to fill your inner being. Praying in tongues is a spiritual battery. It charges you up, and causes you to draw on the love, wisdom, and power of God in your natural life.

> **When you pray in tongues you are having intimate fellowship with God, receiving endurance, confidence, patience, and allowing all of the goodness of God to fill your inner being.**

# Praise and Thanksgiving

If you ever need to encourage yourself and strengthen your faith, then a great place to start is by praising God! God inhabits the praise of His people! Psalms 22:3 (KJV) says, "But thou art holy, *O thou that inhabitest the praises of Israel.*" When you start praising God, He will inhabit the atmosphere around you and fill you up so that you overflow. Some people may think that you can only praise God in church on Sunday, but actually, you can praise God at all times, no matter what is happening around you.

Another way to strengthen your inner man of faith is by giving God thanks for every good thing in your life. The Bible says that you can become more established in your faith and that you can *abound in faith* with thanksgiving. Let's look at a few different Bible translations of Colossians 2:6-7:

> Therefore, as you received Christ Jesus the Lord, so walk in him, rooted and built up in him and **established in the faith**, just as you were taught, **abounding in thanksgiving.** (ESV)

Therefore as you have received Christ Jesus the Lord, walk in [union with] Him [reflecting His character in the things you do and say—living lives that lead others away from sin], having been deeply rooted [in Him] and now being continually built up in Him and **[becoming increasingly more] established in your faith,** just as you were taught, and **overflowing in it with gratitude.** (AMP)

As you therefore have received Christ Jesus the Lord, so walk in Him, rooted and built up in Him and **established in the faith,** as you have been taught, **abounding in it with thanksgiving.** (NKJV)

Thanking God and being thankful causes you to abound in faith! The more thankful you are, the more you will be strong in faith, established in your faith, and able to use your faith as God intended you to! Thanking God is essential to having a victorious Christian life, but wait—there's more! It not only helps you, but it also blesses God and stops the tactics of your spiritual enemy, Satan. Psalm 8:2 (ESV) says, "Out of the mouth of babies and infants, *you have established strength* because of your foes, *to still the enemy and the avenger.*" [3]The word *still* in Hebrew means to repose, desist from exertion; make to cease, make to fail. This verse tells me that you receive inner strength when you are in a place of thankfulness, and you are stopping the plans that the enemy formed against you! Thanking God is a spiritual weapon!

> **You receive inner strength when you are in a place of thankfulness, and you are stopping the plans that the enemy formed against you!**

# Commit Everything to God in Prayer

The Bible also tells you that praise, thanksgiving, and prayer can *transform your life's situations.* These things take your focus off of yourself, and onto God. Philippians 4:4-8 says,

> Always be full of joy in the Lord. I say it again—rejoice! Let everyone see that you are considerate in all you do. Remember, the Lord is coming soon. Don't worry about anything; instead, pray about

everything. Tell God what you need, and thank him for all he has done. Then you will experience God's peace, which exceeds anything we can understand. His peace will guard your hearts and minds as you live in Christ Jesus. And now, dear brothers and sisters, one final thing. Fix your thoughts on what is true, and honorable, and right, and pure, and lovely, and admirable. Think about things that are excellent and worthy of praise.

We can always be full of joy in the Lord because He is good no matter what! God is always worthy of our praise, thanksgiving, and adoration. Take a moment to think through your life. Meditate on how faithful God has been to you.

Has He ever failed you?

I make this a daily practice because thankfulness transformed my heart. I went through a season where I experienced a lot of fear and anxiety. I was desperate to find a refuge from this dark hole that I found myself in. One day, God reminded me of the power of thanksgiving, so I made a list of all the things I was thankful for and hung it on my wall. (This is an exercise that I have in my *Walking in the New You! Workbook,* and I think you'd love it!) This piece of paper hanging on my wall forced me to stop focusing on all the things that filled me with worry and fear. It boldly reminded me of the awesomeness, goodness, and greatness of God. This simple practice shifted my focus, and it healed my heart. Fear and anxiety left me because I filled my heart and mind with the goodness of God.

In my life, I cannot think of one time that God has let me down. Can you? Bad things have happened in my life, but it wasn't God's fault, it was the result of my own choices. Consequences are a real thing; God cannot deliver you from the choices that you make or the choices of the people around you. If you drive 15 mph over the speed limit and get a ticket, then you will have to face that consequence. Or, if your car gets rear-ended by someone who wasn't paying attention, then you will have to face the consequence of their actions. This is why you choose to live your life after God, and make decisions that will glorify Him every day. You will make mistakes along the way, and so will the people around you. That's why you give every area of your life to God so that He can help you and lead you along the way. Commit every negative circumstance to God and He will always turn it around for your good and His glory.

Look at my past, for example. I never believed that I would look at a lifetime of failure, and say that every area has been completely restored, made whole, and is now shining in the brilliance of God.

This puts a HUGE smile on my face because if God can do this for me, He will do it for you! Take heart, dear one, because I didn't do anything other than believe in God and trust Him one step at a time. My life was restored by the powerful love, truth, and grace of God. I just believed in Him and began to make Him the true Lord of my life. As a result, He completely transformed my life.

No matter what you are facing today, you can thank God in advance that He is restoring and redeeming every situation in your life.

We have no need to worry about anything, because we can commit everything to Him in prayer, and know that He hears and answers us. When we ask God for what we need, then we are submitting our life and our will to Him, which is exactly what Jesus told us to do. In Matthew 6:9-10, Jesus instructed us to start our prayers by honoring God first and submitting to His will. From that place of thankful honor and trust, we submit our requests to God knowing that He loves us, takes pleasure in helping us, and delights in our well-being. Prayer is how we commit our most basic and intimate needs to God, and it reveals our trust for Him. The more we trust God, the more we will enter into His presence with boldness in prayer, knowing that He is a good, faithful Father.

And then, God wants to know what you need! The Bible says in multiple places to ask God for what you need. Matthew 7:7-8 (NKJV) says, "Ask, and it will be given to you; seek, and you will find; knock, and it will be opened to you. For everyone who asks receives, and he who seeks finds, and to him who knocks it will be opened." God already knows what you need before you ask Him (Matt. 6:8), but He needs an invitation. This is how God can move on your behalf, as you use your faith to believe Him and ask Him for help. You are giving God an open door into your situation, and this is what He's waiting for! This gives God an opportunity to prove Himself faithful to you, and show Himself strong in your life (2 Chr. 16:9a).

Every day, you can praise God, thank Him for His goodness in your life, and commit your life to Him in prayer. This will cause you to become more established in your faith, abound in faith, and cause the power of God to be evident in your life because you have committed every situation to His trust through prayer. Being thankful is a choice. Trusting God is a choice. When you face each day from a place of thankful trust in God, you will shine from the inside out because God is working through you to make His goodness evident in your life!

> When you choose to be thankful, you will shine from the inside out because God is working through you to make His goodness evident in your life!

And we know [with great confidence] that God [who is deeply concerned about us] causes all things to work together [as a plan] for good for those who love God, to those who are called according to His plan and purpose. (Romans 8:28 AMP)

## Faith Comes by Hearing

Another thing that has greatly impacted my life is *hearing the Word of God.* Whether I'm reading the Bible to myself out loud (which is a daily practice in my life), listening to teachings, or attending church regularly, this has become vital in my walk of faith. This simple principle fills up my inner man of faith, and encourages me in my walk with God. It almost never fails...when I listen to God's Word, I walk away encouraged and strengthened from the inside out because *I'm hearing the anointed Word of God that applies directly to my situation.* I walk away with godly wisdom and insight to handle every situation I face in life. After seeing this happen day after day, year after year, I can approach the hearing of God's Word with awe, reverence, and an expectation to receive something good. Romans 10:17 (NKJV) says, "So then faith comes by hearing, and hearing by the word of God." Faith comes from hearing God's Word. Remember, God's Word is alive, active, and it penetrates the deepest part of your heart and soul (Heb. 4:12). Hearing God's Word awakens the spiritual ears within you, and speaks directly to your inner man. As a result, it will help you to apply what you've heard by the spirit to your natural life. This simple yet powerful principle never fails.

Here are some simple ways that you can hear the Word of God:

1. When you spend time with God, be quiet and ask God to speak to you.
2. Read the Word out loud over yourself.
3. A Bible App can read the Word to you.
4. Attending a church ensures that you are a part of the body of Christ and continually hearing God's Word.
5. A teacher that has resources on TV or the internet that teaches the entire truth in God's Word. For example: Andrew Wommack, Carrie Pickett, Barry

Bennett, Greg Mohr, Duane Sheriff, and Bob Yandian all teach the full gospel written in the Bible. These are some of my favorite teachers that I refer to time and time again for spiritual teaching, wisdom, and encouragement.
6. A mentor or parent in the faith is a practical way to glean every day wisdom and understanding from the Word of God.

Consistently hearing God's Word will ensure that you are being filled up in your spirit. It causes you to be strong in faith, knowing that you've heard from the Spirit of God Himself. This is another way to hear and discern God's direction in your life, so that with every situation you face, you can make decisions based on the greater, spiritual wisdom of God, instead of relying on a limited understanding.

The Bible says in Ephesians 5:26-27 (ESV), "that he might sanctify her, having cleansed her by the *washing of water with the word, so that he might present the church to himself in splendor,* without spot or wrinkle or any such thing, that she might be holy and without blemish." Do you want to live a life full of the splendor of God? I sure do! Hearing God's Word will cleanse you from the inside out, and fill your life with God's glory and splendor. This is how Jesus plans to cleanse and purify the entire body of Christ, one precious saint at a time, to prepare us as His beautiful, holy bride.

> **Hearing God's Word will cleanse you from the inside out, and fill your life with God's glory and splendor.**

Have you ever faced a situation and you were faced with different choices, but you struggled to make the right choice? I certainly have. Now that I know that God is eager to speak to me and lead me through His Word and Spirit, I never have to fear whether or not I'm making the right decision. When I don't know what choice to make, I wait. I spend time with God, praying in tongues, asking Him for wisdom, I pray that His will would be done, and I ask Him to help me make the right decision. I read the Word out loud over myself, declaring it over the situation, and I listen to teachings that will build my faith. After a few minutes or even a couple of days, God always gives me peace that leads me in the course He would have me choose. You never have to wonder if you're making the right choice again! God is on your side and eager to show you the right path. God's path will always lead you to victory!

# Strength to Conceive Your Promise

What are you believing God for today? Take a moment to think about this, and write it down in your journal. Have you been waiting a while? Have you grown weary in your waiting, and had a chance to doubt God's promise for your life? If your answer is "yes" to any of these questions, then let me encourage you. You're right where you're supposed to be! Chances are, that what you've been believing for and waiting for *is* God's promise for your life, and He wants to strengthen your faith while you wait! The Bible says that it requires *faith* and *patience* to inherit the promises. I would like to show you a few different translations for Hebrews 6:11-12:

> Our great desire is that you will **keep on loving others as long as life lasts, in order to make certain that what you hope for will come true.** Then you will not become spiritually dull and indifferent. Instead, you will follow the example of **those who are going to inherit God's promises because of their faith and endurance.** (NLT)

And we desire each one of you to show the same earnestness to have **the full assurance of hope until the end,** so that you may not be sluggish, but imitators of **those who through faith and patience inherit the promises.** (ESV)

And we desire for each one of you to show the same diligence [all the way through] so as to **realize and enjoy the full assurance of hope until the end,** so that you will not be [spiritually] sluggish, but [will instead be] imitators of **those who through faith [lean on God with absolute trust and confidence in Him and in His power] and by patient endurance [even when suffering] are [now] inheriting the promises.** (AMP)

The author of these verses is talking about continuing to love others so that you will stay fully assured in the hope of what you're believing for. Loving others is a key to success in the Christian life. Through your love you will receive hope, and you will be able to stand the test of time as you faithfully wait to inherit the promises of God. Remember, God's promises (His Word) are seeds that can be planted in your heart. After those seeds have had a chance to get rooted in your heart, they will grow up to produce a harvest in your life. Whatever you're believing God for today, keep believing and don't give up. In your waiting, continue to love others and love God, and your hope will carry you through until you receive what you're believing for.

I love the Bible because it is full of instruction on how to live the godly life, with stories that you can relate to, and learn from. One of my favorite examples of faithful endurance is the life of Abraham and Sarah. God's promise to them was to have their own, long-awaited child—a son that would carry on their legacy and fulfill God's purpose for them, the nation of Israel, and eventually for all of mankind (Gen. 12, 15, 17). *It took 25 years for Abraham and Sarah to receive their promise.* My question is, why did it take so long? Maybe it was the appointed time for Isaac to be born. Maybe God needed their faith to be on board with what He was trying to do in their life. I may not know the full answer to this question in my lifetime, but I can learn from their experience which God has provided through His Word. The Bible says that Abraham believed God (Rom. 4:3), but that Sarah laughed at God's promise.

> Now Abraham and Sarah were old, advanced in years. The way of women had ceased to be with Sarah. So Sarah laughed to herself, saying, "After I

am worn out, and my lord is old, shall I have pleasure?" The LORD said to Abraham, "Why did Sarah laugh and say, 'Shall I indeed bear a child, now that I am old?' Is anything too hard for the LORD? At the appointed time I will return to you, about this time next year, and Sarah shall have a son." But Sarah denied it, saying, "I did not laugh," for she was afraid. He said, "No, but you did laugh."
(Genesis 18:11-15 ESV)

First, I would like to cover *what not to do.* Sarah was old in age, and well past child-bearing years, which in her eyes was something that God couldn't overcome. She had her eyes on the circumstances of the natural realm instead of the awesomeness, goodness, and power of God. As a result, she mocked God by laughing at *the promise, the potential, and the purpose* He had for her life. God responded to her unbelief and asked, "Is anything too hard for the Lord?" (Gen. 18:14). This is a good lesson to learn from. Is there a situation in your life that seems impossible? Maybe you are looking at it, scoffing in disbelief, and thinking that your situation will never change. If so, I would take this time to acknowledge the goodness of God towards you, and repent for your unbelief. *Shift your focus to God's ability working on your behalf, doing the impossible in your life.*

Whenever your eyes are on the natural limitations, then you are not acknowledging the truth about who you are in Christ and who He is in you. To walk in the powerful fullness of your new identity, you must shift your attention to Him, and believe that He can, and will, move mountains on your behalf. When you believe that God is bringing forth your purpose by doing the impossible for you, then you will see the greatness of His promises, and you will discover the massive amount of potential that your life carries. Once you get on board with God by believing His perfect plan for your life, He will be able to propel you further into your destiny.

> **When you believe that God is bringing forth your purpose by doing the impossible for you, then you will see the greatness of His promises, and you will discover the massive amount of potential that your life carries.**

Second, I would like to talk about *what to do*. The Bible says that Abraham, on the other hand, was *strong in faith* because he *believed God, he was not considering the natural circumstances, and he was fully convinced that God would do what He said He would do* (Rom. 4:17-22). This is a perfect example of how we should approach every promise from God. The Bible says in 2 Corinthians 1:20-22,

> For all of God's promises have been fulfilled in Christ with a resounding "Yes!" And through Christ, our "Amen" (which means "Yes") ascends to God for his glory. It is God who enables us, along with you, to stand firm for Christ. He has commissioned us, and he has identified us as his own by placing the Holy Spirit in our hearts as the first installment that guarantees everything he has promised us.

Every promise in God's Word is for you, and because of Jesus Christ you can say with Him, "Yes, I receive that promise by faith! Amen!" When you agree with God by saying, "yes and amen," to His goodness towards you, then you are activating spiritual substance within you to come into the natural realm. All of the blessings of God are in your spirit, ready for you to believe them, wake them up, and draw them out. God has already accomplished the payment of it for you by the blood of His Son. And to help you believe that every good thing is for you, God has given you the Holy Spirit within you as a guarantee. Nothing and no one can separate you from the goodness of God in Christ

Jesus because you are sealed with the Holy Spirit. Every blessing is yours in Christ (Eph. 1:3). You don't have to waiver and wonder if God is for you, and if He has good plans for you. You are marked with His name, sealed with His Spirit, and promised every spiritual blessing in Christ Jesus! The only one who can stop you from receiving it is you, through your wavering and inability to believe it.

Which leads us back to Sarah. Eventually, Sarah got to a point where she was using her faith, because the Bible says in Hebrews 11:11 (NKJV),

> **By faith** Sarah herself also **received strength to conceive** seed, and she bore a child when she was past the age, **because she judged Him faithful who had promised.**

You see from this verse that *by faith* Sarah *received strength to conceive God's promise* in her life *because she judged God faithful.* Faith gives you strength to conceive God's promise. Sarah got her eyes off of the circumstances, off of what her body was saying, off of what her mind and heart were saying, and she believed in her heart and used her faith. As a result, she became strong in faith and that gave her strength to conceive God's promise.

> **Faith gives you strength to conceive God's promise.**

I can relate to Sarah. For many years, I was single. Some days I wanted to be married, and some days I didn't. I greatly desired to be married, but because it hadn't come to pass, doubt persuaded me to disbelieve. I thought, *does God really want this for me? Maybe I should just stay single for the rest of my life.* It was an attempt to protect my heart from further disappointment, but it caused me to be wavy and double-minded. Sometimes, I trusted and believed that the desire in my heart to be married was a desire that God placed within me, and sometimes I doubted.

> But let him ask in faith, with no doubting, for he who doubts is like a wave of the sea driven and tossed by the wind. For let not that man suppose that he will receive anything from the Lord; he is a double-minded man, unstable in all his ways.
> (James 1:6-8 NKJV)

Ouch. I was definitely being double-minded and wavering. This verse says that when I'm double-minded, then I shouldn't expect to receive anything from the Lord.

God wants me to be fully persuaded that He is able to bring forth the desires in my heart no matter how impossible or far away they may seem. That way, I won't try to do it in my own strength, and He will get all the glory for being so good! God spoke that verse to me in January of 2020. He said, "If you want this promise to come to pass, then I need you to determine in your heart that this is what you want, and that I will accomplish it for you." So I finally got on board with God. In my heart, I determined these things:

1. I believe this is God's will for me.
2. I will glorify God and thank Him for His promise to me.
3. I want this, and I will continue to want this...even when it doesn't come to pass right away.
4. I believe that God will bring this to pass at the right time.
5. I wrote down verses that God had given me regarding my future husband and confessed these truths with my mouth every day.

This is how I persuaded my heart in the promises of God. I drew a line in the sand and determined that this is God's will, that I am going to use my faith with all of my heart and mind, and that God will honor His promise to me.

Whenever my heart tried to condemn me or question God's goodness towards me, I reminded myself of the awesomeness and goodness of God's will towards me, and spoke the truth out of my mouth.

Within a few months, God began to speak to me about my good friend, Greg Weisbrodt. God was opening my mind and heart to the idea of "more than friendship" with Greg, and asking if I would be interested in a lifelong relationship with this man of God. Greg and I had been close friends for three years, and he was a great brother in Christ. I had seen this man of God model faithfulness, godly strength, diligence, and a passionate pursuit of God in his daily life for several years. After weeks and months of prayer, counsel, and consideration, I opened my heart to the idea, and God began to confirm that this was His will, His promise to me. Even then, God was waiting for me to get on board with Him, and to discover for myself if this is what I wanted. God will never force His promises upon us, but He will wait for us to discover them, agree with them, and believe them, so that we can receive strength to conceive them in our life. Greg and I were married that same year. The same year that I decided to thank God in advance for His goodness towards me, to be fully persuaded in my heart, and to speak forth my faith, was the year that I received my promise.

When God makes a promise to you, don't look at the natural realm for proof of God's faithfulness. God will always be faithful no matter what your circumstances say. If your life doesn't match the promises in God's Word, then keep believing God. You can follow these same principles for anything that you're believing for. God's promises will stand the test of time and they are always "yes and amen" for you.

Your faith is spiritual matter that brings the promises in God's Word into your natural life! No matter what, keep relying on the grace of God working for you through your faith in Him. You can build yourself up on your most holy faith by praying in tongues, being thankful, committing your life to God in prayer, and by consistently filling yourself up through the hearing of God's Word. These simple things will fill up your "belief" tank, and drain your "unbelief" tank, which will give you strength to conceive every promise in God's Word. Always keep your eyes on Jesus, the Author and Finisher of your faith (Heb. 12:2). If God has given you faith to believe for something, then He will help you accomplish it, and bring it to pass in your life!

> **If God has given you faith to believe for something, then He will help you accomplish it, and bring it to pass in your life!**

# Transform Your Life
## Application of Chapter Concepts

**A Moment of Reflection: Living a Prosperous Life**

1. Does it change your opinion of faith knowing that you have been given the faith of God?
    - If so, how does this impact your faith currently?

2. Out of the faith strengthening points that were discussed, which ones stood out to you the most?
    - Are there any that you feel led to incorporate in your life? Here is a list to help jog your memory:
        1. Grace and faith
        2. Praying in tongues
        3. Praise and thanksgiving
        4. Commit everything to God in prayer
        5. Faith comes by hearing
        6. Strength to conceive your promise

3. How can you incorporate praying in tongues into your day more?
    - I encourage you to pray in tongues as much as you can. It will strengthen you from the inside out!

4. Praise, thanksgiving, prayer, and hearing God's Word are powerful spiritual tools! How would you like to incorporate those principles into your life more?
    - In my life, I set aside the first part of my day to lift my hands and praise God. Next, I thank Him for every good thing in my life, and I pray in tongues, knowing that I am giving thanks well (1 Cor. 14:17). Then, I pray and talk to God about what's going on in my life. I spend time being quiet, and I invite Him to speak to me. Finally, I ask Him to lead me to a chapter to read, and I read it out loud, pausing to meditate on the passage, and giving Him space to speak to my heart.
    - Sometimes, it can be easy to get into a spiritual "routine" that can become religious and ineffective. Remember, it's

about your relationship with God; fellowship and friendship. Let Holy Spirit lead you in your routine with Him! Invite Him every morning to fill you afresh, help you, and lead you.

5. Spend time alone with God, and let Him guide your heart. What is the next step of faith that you can take in these areas? What do you sense He is leading you to do next? Listen to His voice, and write down thoughts that come to your mind. Remember, God's voice will always agree with the Word. If a thought comes that contradicts God's Word, you can replace it with the truth.

## My Transformation Scripture

What is a scripture that speaks to you about being strong in faith? Meditate on this verse throughout the day, and remind yourself of the power of your faith. Here are several suggestions:
- Strengthened with all might, according to His glorious power, for all patience and long suffering with joy. (Colossians 1:11 NKJV)

- And His name, through faith in His name, has made this man strong, whom you see and know. Yes, the faith which comes through Him has given him this perfect soundness in the presence of you all. (Acts 3:16 NKJV)
- Stand firm against him, and be strong in your faith. Remember that your family of believers all over the world is going through the same kind of suffering you are. (1 Peter 5:9)
- Be on guard. Stand firm in the faith. Be courageous. Be strong. (1 Corinthians 16:13)
- Abraham never wavered in believing God's promise. In fact, his faith grew stronger, and in this he brought glory to God. (Romans 4:20)
- By faith Sarah herself received power to conceive, even when she was past the age, since she considered him faithful who had promised. (Hebrews 11:11)
- Therefore, as you received Christ Jesus the Lord, so walk in him, rooted and built up in him and established in the faith, just as you were taught, abounding in thanksgiving. (Colossians 2:6-7)

Write the scripture that you chose in your journal.

### Time in His Presence

Spend some time with God meditating on your transformation scripture. What do you think the Lord is speaking to you through this verse?

### Life Application

Ask Holy Spirit to help you apply this scripture to your daily life. How can I apply this to my life today?

### Prayer

If you acknowledge that God has given you His faith to save you, strengthen you, and redeem your life from destruction, then please pray with me:

*God, thank You for Jesus! Thank You for giving me Your faith! I acknowledge the truth about who I am in the spirit. Help me to strengthen my faith so I can use it effectively. Reveal any areas in my life where I'm not believing You with my whole heart. Show me how to incorporate these principles into my life so that I can fellowship with You, and be more like You, Lord. I love You. Thank You so much for every good thing You've given me! I receive Your promises with a giant, Yes and Amen! In Jesus' name. Amen.*

# Chapter 11

## Ruled by the Spirit

### Strengthening Your Inner Man

*Those who live only to satisfy their own sinful nature will harvest decay and death from that sinful nature. But those who live to please the Spirit will harvest everlasting life from the Spirit.*
—Galatians 6:8

After several years of practice and learning how to use my faith effectively, I finally understood what the Bible means when it says that we can live by the Spirit.

> Those who are dominated by the sinful nature think about sinful things, but those who are controlled by the Holy Spirit think about things that please the Spirit. So letting your sinful nature control your mind leads to death. But letting the Spirit control your mind leads to life and peace. (Romans 8:5-6)

I was beginning to experience a life dominated by the Spirit because I had surrendered every area of my life to God. I gave Him my spirit, my soul, my body, my will, my emotions, my finances, my health, my career, my relationships. I began to trust God and believe Him in every way imaginable, and I relied on Him for my every need. This doesn't mean that I never had a flesh flash, that I did everything perfectly, or that I never had a problem. To this day, I literally cry out and weep to God at least once a week because I did something wrong and I need His help! This just means that I continually go back to God, and rely on Him in every situation. This complete and utter reliance on God not only caused my inner man of faith to be strengthened, but it set my life free. I was no longer tempted with comparison, lack, depression, poverty, or envy. I was set free to believe in Christ in me the hope of glory—that I have every spiritual blessing in Christ, and that I can accomplish all things with Him! These truths were becoming a part of me and transformed how I lived my life each day. My life began to thrive because I was constantly relying on the Spirit to direct me, instead of relying on my wavering feelings to support me and comfort me.

This constant fellowship and reliance upon God enables you to live in the spirit, feed your spirit, and cultivate an inviting atmosphere for the Spirit of God to prosper your life. This is a life ruled by the Spirit, filled with His wisdom and ability, and transformed by His presence.

# Natural Results from a Spiritual Adjustment

The natural realm is a reflection of what is happening in the spirit (Prov. 23:7). If you want to change the results you see in your life, then I encourage you to evaluate how you're spending your time, the words that you're speaking, and where you're spending your money. Spend time with God and the Word, so that you can align your life with your born again spirit. Your spirit is identical to Jesus Christ! You don't need to become righteous through your actions—you are righteous as soon as you make Jesus your Lord and Savior. In order to align your life with the truth of who you are in the spirit, you may need to make some adjustments.

Proverbs 4:18 says, "The way of the righteous is like the first gleam of dawn, which shines ever brighter until the full light of day." The life of the righteous gets brighter and brighter until Jesus returns! God promises that your life will get better and better and better when you follow Him and His ways.

> **The natural realm is a reflection of what is happening in the spirit.**

I remember when I went to England to do a discipleship training school. I thought that I would arrive, sit around, and learn about God. Boy, was I wrong! While attending the school, you had to get up early, participate, do chores, attend lectures, minister to people on the street, talk in front of the classroom, and practice applying the Word of God to your life every day. One day specifically, we were all getting ready to leave England after the three-month learning phase, and go to the Philippines for the two-month application phase. This is where the rubber meets the road, and you get hands on training for all the things you just learned. During this time, you discover if you're truly meant to be a missionary.

There were about thirty of my classmates, myself, and an instructor in this upper room for class. We were there to pray for our future mission trip and the people we would be ministering to. I remember sitting there, praying in tongues, occasionally praying with my understanding, but I was tired. I really wasn't into it. I was there physically, but I was asleep spiritually. I remember our instructor, Elle. She was tough. She was as strong as horseradish in the spirit. I think she could sense that my classmates and I weren't putting in much effort. In a loud voice, she announced from the front of the room, "Get up! All of you! Stand up! Walk around the room if you need to, but you need to wake up your spirit man! Pray in the spirit!"

It was like she was giving each of us a charge in the spirit and saying, "You need to wake up your spirit man and fight because you are headed into a spiritual war. You need to be ready!" And she was right. That two-month mission trip in the Philippines was one of the hardest times in my life in many ways.

Even to this day, I think about Elle when I'm having quiet time. When my body and soul are tired and weak, my spirit is awake, ready and willing. I just need to wake it up.

# Wake Up Your Spirit

"So be on your guard, not asleep like the others. Stay alert and be clearheaded" (1 Thes. 5:6). Other translations say to "watch and be sober," which is talking about in your mind, soul, and spirit; to be sober minded and awake spiritually, and in every part of your being. This chapter goes on to say, "But let us who are of the day be sober, putting on the breastplate of faith and love, and as an helmet the hope of salvation" (vv 8, NKJV). There are a few things I'd like to expand on in this verse. The first is the breastplate. The breastplate is defensive armor that covers your heart and the most vital organs in the body. The faith and love of God is your breastplate that should always be guarding your heart—your source of life. Faith and love remind you of who you are in the spirit, and who Christ is in you. The Bible is continually nudging you towards love. I'm sure you're familiar with the famous love chapter in the Bible, which states,

> If I had the gift of prophecy, and if I understood all of God's secret plans and possessed all knowledge, and if I had such faith that I could move mountains, but didn't love others, I would be nothing.
> (1 Corinthians 13:2)

We may have a strong faith that can move mountains, but without love, it doesn't mean anything. Which moves us to the second point I'd like to make: hope. Maintaining your hope in God will help you to stir up and strengthen your spirit. The second part of 1 Thessalonians 5:8 (NKJV) says, "...putting on...and as a helmet the hope of salvation." *The hope of salvation as a helmet provides protection for your mind.* It reminds you that Christ paid for more than your eternal destiny, but a life of health, healing, abundance, and deliverance.

---

**When you are keeping the truth in the forefront of your mind, you will remain spiritually strengthened and stirred up as Christ's soldier.**

---

So when something comes to your mind that is contrary to this, you can disregard it completely, and refocus your attention to things that are hopeful, praiseworthy, and good. Christ paid for your complete freedom on this earth, which is obtained through your spirit, or inner man.

To keep your spirit strengthened, awake, and stirred up, you can activate your mind to think on spiritual things. Your mind must be agreeing with God in order to dominate your soul and spirit. When you are keeping the truth in the forefront of your mind and heart, you will remain spiritually strengthened and stirred up as Christ's soldier. This is an essential practice if you want to endure hardness and keep your faith until Christ returns again.

The last point I would like to make regarding stirring up your spirit is this: all three of these things are tied together. Do you remember the verses in Hebrews 6 that I covered in Chapter 10; that your love for others is tied to your hope? Well, I am going to highlight one more verse from that chapter.

For God is not unjust. He will not forget how hard you have worked for him and how you have **shown your love to him by caring for other believers**, as you still do. Our great desire is that you will keep on loving others as long as life lasts, in order **to make certain that what you hope for will come true.** Then you will not become spiritually dull and indifferent. Instead, you will follow the example of **those who are going to inherit God's promises because of their faith and endurance.** (Hebrews 6:10-12)

We love God when we care for other believers and other people. The more we lay down our life to lovingly serve other people, the more we will abound in hope and faith. Our love towards others is directly connected to our hope staying alive and our faith staying strong.

---

**Our love towards others is directly connected to our hope staying alive and our faith staying strong.**

---

Several years into my Christian walk, I was wounded by people in the church, and I wanted to disconnect from the body of Christ and do my own thing. I wanted life to be all about me and God; all about His purpose for my life, and who cares about anyone else. Well, we can see from the life of Jesus that that is not God's will for us. God intends to save the lost, deliver them from the pain of living in a captivity of sin and destruction, and completely restore their life so that they can go out and tell others the good news! God didn't save me from my sin so that I could hole up in a cave and be blessed all by myself. He wants His blessing and goodness to shine from our lives so that when an unbeliever sees how good life can be, that they want what we have. God is the only explanation for living such an amazing life of wholeness, completeness, and excellence—we lack no good thing. God had to work on my character, and let me know that *other people are so important to Him.* Bringing forth unity and love in the body of Christ is an essential charge to every believer's faith, whether they know it or not. So, we need to have faith, hope, and love for others if we want our lives to shine with the brightness of God's goodness and glory.

> Three things will last forever—faith, hope, and love—and the greatest of these is love.
> (1 Corinthians 13:13)

If we want to be stirred up in the spirit, protecting our heart with faith and love, and guarding our minds with the hope of the gospel, then we must choose to intentionally love others at all times. Once I understood this, and developed an intentional love towards others, my faith and hope became alive within me. I stayed stirred up in the spirit at all times, no matter what came against me! Sometimes, we may need to remind ourselves to wake up our spirit man...make ourselves stand up and fight in the spirit like Elle. I think that Elle knew what she was talking about, and I'm so glad that she woke me up!

I will never forget that simple practice of standing up, praying in tongues, and doing some spiritual exercise so that my spirit can rule over my flesh. The good news of Jesus Christ is worth "staying awake" for. If I want to finish my race with strength, I must stay awake.

## The Flesh versus the Spirit

Your spirit is identical to Jesus Christ. As He is right now, so are you in this world (1 John 4:17). Since Jesus has been given all power and authority, so has your spirit. Therefore, your spirit always has authority over your flesh. The Bible refers to the flesh as your natural man, which is your soul and body. This part of you is usually led by your mind, will, emotions, and your five senses: see, taste, hear, smell, and feel. The Bible also calls this, *the carnal man.* It talks to you by saying, I'm hungry, feed me; or put me to bed, I'm tired; or I'm emotional and sad. This is not a bad part of you—this is good! God created you to be this way. Your soul and body will tell you things to let you know what's going on around you. These are natural instincts that God gave you to help you survive and to keep you alive in this mortal body. These natural instincts are also directly related to your old, sinful nature, that passed away when you got born again. It's important that you no longer let your fleshly, sinful nature dominate your life, but rather, to be led by the Spirit in all things. Let's look at some verses together.

**So I say, let the Holy Spirit guide your lives. Then you won't be doing what your sinful nature craves.** The sinful nature wants to do evil, which is just the opposite of what the Spirit wants. **And the Spirit gives us desires that are the opposite of what the sinful nature desires. These two forces are constantly fighting each other, so you are not free to carry out your good intentions.** But when you are directed by the Spirit, you are not under obligation to the law of Moses. **When you follow the desires of your sinful nature, the results are very clear: sexual immorality, impurity, lustful pleasures, idolatry, sorcery, hostility, quarreling, jealousy, outbursts of anger, selfish ambition, dissension, division, envy,**

**drunkenness, wild parties, and other sins like these.** Let me tell you again, as I have before, that **anyone living that sort of life will not inherit the Kingdom of God. But the Holy Spirit produces this kind of fruit in our lives: love, joy, peace, patience, kindness, goodness, faithfulness, gentleness, and self-control.** There is no law against these things! Those who belong to Christ Jesus have nailed the passions and desires of their sinful nature to his cross and crucified them there. **Since we are living by the Spirit, let us follow the Spirit's leading in every part of our lives.** (Galatians 5:16-25)

We all have these two forces within us: our new, born again nature (our spirit) versus our old, sinful nature (our flesh). Our flesh will always be contrary to the things of God (vv 17), which is why we don't want to be dominated or led by our flesh.

Can you think back through your life, and remember a time when you were led by your flesh? Did that choice lead to good consequences, or bad ones?

I remember as a young child stealing a toy and lying to my parents about it! The rest of my life followed a very similar pattern. I took part in everything on that sinful nature list in Galatians 5: "...sexual immorality, impurity, lustful pleasures, idolatry, sorcery, hostility, quarreling, jealousy, outbursts of anger, selfish ambition, dissension, division, envy, drunkenness, wild parties, and other sins like these..." (vv 19-21). The things that aren't on this list, I also partook in: abortion, mutilation, homosexuality, jails, suicide, hatred, and violence. Every time I gave in to my sinful desires, I remember waking up in the morning with a pit in my stomach, feeling so guilty for what I had done. But I didn't know there was another way to live. I had lost hope for my life and my choices were a direct result of my ignorance.

One glorious day of my journey, I was two weeks in to my 30-day sentence at an inpatient treatment center. Not allowed to leave, constantly monitored, and forced to be sober, I was walking down the sidewalk in the sun. Everything hit me at once as I awoke from the fog I had been living under. I stopped in my tracks and thought to myself, *what have I done? I have completely destroyed my life, and I have no idea how to get it back.* I felt that pit in my stomach all over again, terrified to face the consequences that laid before me. But this time was different. This time, I gave in to that feeling, and surrendered to it instead of pushing it away. Now I was in a place where the Holy Spirit could work with me. That one moment of surrender allowed Holy Spirit to lead me and guide me. He led me to discover the truth where I realized that God is real, that He wants to be in a relationship with me, and that all my sins are instantly forgiven through my faith in Jesus Christ. Who wouldn't want to be in a relationship with a God like that?

To live life by the Spirit instead of your flesh is just a simple, internal act of surrender. It's so easy to dismiss, but so vital to living life with God. Whenever you feel a pit, a hole, or an empty place in your stomach, lean into God instead of pushing Him away. That feeling is there for a reason; it's your conscience leading you to a better way— His way.

> **To live life by the Spirit instead of your flesh is just a simple, internal act of surrender.**

## Led by the Spirit

After reading this, you may be asking, "How do I know if I'm being led by my flesh or by my spirit?" The Bible says, "But you are not controlled by your sinful nature. You are controlled by the Spirit if you have the Spirit of God living in you. (And remember that those who do not have the Spirit of Christ living in them do not belong to him at all)" (Rom. 8:9). This verse tells you that if you are born again, then you are always led by the Spirit! The Holy Spirit is leading you, you just have to learn how to listen.

The Holy Spirit's job within you is to help you! He is constantly guiding you to God's best for you. The Holy Spirit will lead you by your desires, and by small "nudges" in your heart. Holy Spirit is your Helper, your moral compass, and your conscience; He is leading you to God's perfect will for your life! The Holy Spirit is the still small voice within you that helps you make decisions.

> The Spirit of God, who raised Jesus from the dead, lives in you. And just as God raised Christ Jesus from the dead, he will give life to your mortal bodies by this same Spirit living within you. Therefore, dear brothers and sisters, you have no obligation to do what your sinful nature urges you to do. For if you live by its dictates, you will die. But if through the power of the Spirit you put to death the deeds of your sinful nature, you will live. (Romans 8:11-13)

When you listen to Holy Spirit and obey His leadings, then He will give you His strength and power to accomplish it. All you have to do is decide in your heart to obey Him.

The more you listen to His leading and obey Him, the louder His leadings will become, and the easier it will be for you to follow Him instead of your flesh.

## Feed Your Spirit

Feeding your spirit is the opposite of feeding your flesh. In order to feed your spirit, you may need to turn off some distractions. I have noticed that when Holy Spirit draws me to spend time with Him, my flesh always wants to do something different. When I listen to my flesh, I always feel empty afterwards or spiritually depleted. When I listen to my spirit, I always feel full of life, and spiritually charged.

> **When you listen to the Holy Spirit and obey His leadings, then He will give you His strength and power to accomplish it.**

Let's say I were to tell you to go watch TV for two hours, eat junk food, and let your mind think about anything it wants to. Two hours later, you would come back to me and say, "I feel horrible inside and out." I've seen this in my life and other people's lives hundreds of times. Let's say I tell you to go read your Bible, pray in tongues, and thank God for two hours. Two hours later, you would come back to me and say, "Wow! I feel so full of life! God loved me, spoke to me, filled me with direction, and gave me energy to get things accomplished!"

This is what God does when we spend time with Him. When we feed our spirit, we are feeding the life of God in us, which always fills us with divine strength, energy, and wisdom. This is the only explanation I have for the divine strength, health, favor, blessing, and ability that God has graced my life with. I don't take credit for these things in any way, and I completely acknowledge that this is God alone! I love to start my day with God, and I set apart this time for Him, so that I am filled up and fed in the Spirit, and ready to conquer the day with Him. This is a beautiful relationship that continually draws us to be with Him. Every time we choose to be alone with God, we will be filled up, charged up, and empowered to do great things with Him!

## The Presence of the Spirit

As a child of God, it is vital to cultivate an atmosphere of *reverence for God's presence.* A present-day culture of busyness and an increasing amount of responsibilities can creep in to steal the presence of God from your home. Beware! Jesus paid for you to be able to enter the presence of God whenever you want to. Don't take this for granted. Don't mistake the quietness and gentleness of Holy Spirit's leading as Him not speaking to you. Even though Holy Spirit's leadings are precious and gentle, He is also jealous of your time (James 4:5), and He is still Lord of all creation.

> **When you feed your spirit, you are feeding the life of God within you, which always fills you with divine strength, energy, and wisdom.**

There is a cautious balance that we must be aware of. As believers, we should not become too familiar with God so that we ignore Him when He leads us. If our boss walked in the room, I would hope that we all make sure we're on our best behavior—not texting on our phones, scrolling social media, or being sloppy or lazy. I think most of us would agree on that. That's because we have a proper view of authority, integrity, and a righteous fear and reverence for our boss. Just because God can't be seen physically doesn't mean He's not there. God is always with us, watching us, and leading us. Our ears should constantly be tuned into Him, waiting for Him to speak, waiting for Him to lead us, so that the moment He does, we are ready to obey. That is what a holy fear and reverence for God will produce our lives. God is the utmost High King and Lord of our life. When He speaks, we obey. When He says "stop," we stop. He deserves every ounce of our affection; our complete awe, wonder, glory, and respect. The more time that we spend in His presence, the more we will discover His multi-faceted character. We will see Him as God, yes, but we will also encounter Him as our Lord, Father, Provider, Friend, Husband, Protector, Healer, Counselor, Teacher, Brother, Helper, Comforter, Prince, King, Almighty One, the I AM. God is holy. God is holy. *God is holy.*

    Being in His presence is special and not to be taken for granted. When the Holy Spirit meets with you and you receive one touch, one glimpse of His glory, you cannot contain it. His goodness overwhelms you in the best possible way, and suddenly you are aware that you just encountered the presence of God. God is everything that you need, and relationship with Him is the only way that you can accomplish the impossible in your life. Whatever that "impossible" is for you...He's enough, and He's the only answer—always.

    Do you have a need? God is the answer. Holy Spirit is always speaking and drawing you to His presence, so that He can help you accomplish what you can't do on your own.

God is the Author of your life. Time with Him is the only thing that will satisfy the life you've been given. To create a welcoming atmosphere for God, invite Holy Spirit to come and spend time with you and your family. When you make room for Him by spending time with Him, He reveals Himself quickly and readily, excited to show you the Father's heart. He will speak to your heart, and fill you with the wisdom of God to lead you to the answers you need. His presence will heal your life, marriage, relationships, heart, emotions, and body because you are spending time with the Life Source Himself. God is always trying to lead you to wholeness in every area of your life. Instead of pushing away that drawing within you, give in to it. He has placed a hunger for God inside of each person because He created you in His image to be in a relationship with Him. Your purpose on this earth is to be in relationship with God! Time in the presence of God will satisfy your every longing and fulfill your every need. From that relationship, you will find the answers for everything else you need in life.

---

**Time in the presence of God will satisfy your every longing and fulfill your every need.**

Seek the Kingdom of God above all else, and live righteously, and he will give you everything you need. (Matthew 6:33)

# The Life-Giving Spirit

Let me ask you a question, and please be honest with yourself. Do you feel *alive* every day? When you get out of bed in the morning, do you look forward to the day ahead, or do you face dread and fear? Do you feel like your life is *thriving?* Do you feel *full of life, overflowing,* and *abounding* in every corner of your existence? Look into your heart. Search yourself. What areas feel like they're hurting, lacking, or less than an abundant life? I'm not asking this question to shame you or make you feel condemned. I'm asking so that I can fill you with the hope of God. God offers life and freedom to any area that feels less than a *full, thriving, abundant life.* John 6:63 (ESV) says, "It is the Spirit who gives life; the flesh is no help at all. The words that I have spoken to you are spirit and life." John 10:10 says, "The thief's purpose is to steal and kill and destroy. My purpose is to give them a rich and satisfying life." God desires to give you a rich and satisfying life through His Word and Spirit. The Spirit and Word of God *will bring life to you.* What kind of *life* am I talking about? A life that is full, complete, free, perfect, peaceful, satisfied, prospering, content, blessed, overflowing, thriving, lacking nothing, healed, whole, joyful, passionate, purposeful, intentional, and the list can go on! This is the promise of the life of Jesus Christ living in you and through you. This is the life you live when you live by the Spirit and Word of God. It transforms every area of your life from the inside out.

Sometimes, it feels difficult to fully explain the treasures contained within a life devoted to the Spirit of God. I've experienced it, but I'm yet to find the best words to explain it in an understandable way. Throughout the pages of the Bible, I've discovered countless sweet, precious encounters with God, as my ordinary space becomes transformed by His holy presence. I love the way that the authors of the different books of the Bible come together with each of their own individual expressions after they have encountered God. Some faint because of the fear and terror they experienced in His presence. Others shout and rejoice. Some write love songs in an attempt to express their pounding heart that beats only for the One True God. I love the way that the Book of Proverbs combines wisdom that you can apply to your daily life matched with untold reverence for our amazing Creator. It's an instruction book to the believer, and it gives you insight on how to walk in the wisdom of God's Word and Spirit. I have included Proverbs 3:1-18 (TPT) so that you can see the promises of wholeness and blessing to those who live their life devoted to God and being led by His Spirit.

# The Rewards of Wisdom

1-2 My child, if you truly want a long and satisfying life, never forget the things that I've taught you. Follow closely every truth that I've given you. Then you will have a full, rewarding life.

3 Hold on to loyal love and don't let go, and be faithful to all that you've been taught. Let your life be shaped by integrity, with truth written upon your heart.

4 That's how you will find favor and understanding with both God and men—you will gain the reputation of living life well.

**Wisdom's Guidance**

5 Trust in the Lord completely, and do not rely on your own opinions. With all your heart rely on him to guide you, and he will lead you in every decision you make.

6 Become intimate with him in whatever you do,
   and he will lead you wherever you go.
7 Don't think for a moment that you know it all,
   for wisdom comes when you adore him with undivided devotion and avoid everything that's wrong.
8 Then you will find the healing refreshment
   your body and spirit long for.
9 Glorify God with all your wealth, honoring him with your first fruits, with every increase that comes to you.
10 Then every dimension of your life will overflow with blessings from an uncontainable source of inner joy!

**Wisdom's Correction**

11 My child, when the Lord God speaks to you,
   never take his words lightly, and never be upset when he corrects you.
12 For the Father's discipline comes only from his passionate love and pleasure for you. Even when it seems like his correction is harsh, it's still better than any father on earth gives to his child.
13 Blessings pour over the ones who find wisdom,
   for they have obtained living-understanding.

14 As wisdom increases, a great treasure is imparted, greater than many bars of refined gold.

15 It is a more valuable commodity than gold and gemstones, for there is nothing you desire that could compare to her.

16 Wisdom extends to you long life in one hand and wealth and promotion in the other. Out of her mouth flows righteousness, and her words release both law and mercy.

17 The ways of wisdom are sweet, always drawing you into the place of wholeness.

18 Seeking for her brings the discovery of untold blessings, for she is the healing tree of life to those who taste her fruits.

If someone would have told me 12 years ago that one day I would live the type of life that Proverbs 3 promises—a life of wholeness, serenity, joy, and freedom—I wouldn't have believed them. Wherever you are standing today, I'm here to tell you that this type of life is possible for you, too. The Spirit and Word of God will always produce life within you: a life that is long, full of life, joy, pleasures, health, and happiness. The more you eat healthy food, the more it will change your body. The more you feast on the Word, the more it will change your soul and feed your spirit. The more you feed your flesh, the more your sinful nature will dominate your life. Give attention to and feed the one you want to rule. Starve the one you want to silence.

> **The Spirit and Word of God will always produce life within you: a life that is long, full of life, joy, pleasures, health, and happiness.**

## Lights, Camera, Action!

In the fall of 2022, God opened a door for me to be on live television through the ministry I work for. Anyone who knows me knows that I am a behind-the-scenes type of woman. I enjoy being "the helper." That is my gift. Nor do I like being the center of attention, in the spotlight, or for parties to be held in my favor. I am an introvert, I adore small groups of people, and one-on-one get-togethers the most. So when this door opened for me, it felt like someone sucked all the air out of the room and left none for me.

I immediately took it to the throne room with my Father, and sought His will for me. "God, what do you want me to do?" My husband and I took three days to pray and bring it before God. By the end of the weekend, I knew that it was God's will for me to walk through this door and accept the offer. Naturally, I was shaking in my boots. In my spirit, I had peace. So, I said "yes" to this opportunity, and trusted that God had a purpose in it.

During the first live TV shoot, I experienced a lot of physical symptoms. Before it started, I was so nervous that I thought I was either going to pass out or die. Either one would have saved me from what I was feeling at that moment. The lights were shining in my eyes. People were standing around talking, and acting like everything was normal. All I could do was just breathe, and focus on staying vertical while smiling. In the midst of all this, I trusted God more than what I felt, and I kept going. I didn't die. I didn't pass out. God showed Himself faithful through my obedience to trust Him. Day after day after day, I continued to show up and do what God told me to do, even though my flesh was screaming at me every time. It was hard to sleep. Hard to relax even. But I kept going, knowing that this was my Father's best for me.

I continued to seek God and ask Him, "Are you sure this is what you want me to do? Why isn't this getting easier for me?" My flesh was weak, but in my spirit I still had a willing peace. I knew that He had a reason for me doing these live TV episodes.

Today, I can say that I actually look forward to them. Through these live TV episodes, I enjoy getting to love the audience, love God, rely on Holy Spirit, and honor the teachers I work with. I know that this isn't about me—it's all for the glory of Jesus Christ, and to spread the gospel around the world. The fact that I got so nervous for those live TV episodes tells me that I had a lot of pride that needed to be broken off of my life. If I want to be a surrendered vessel for the Lord and obey anything He tells me to do, then I need to be more concerned with His will than my comfort. If obeying God makes my flesh a little uncomfortable here and there, good. I would rather do what God is asking me to do and glorify Him through my life, than stay safe and comfortable. I still don't have a full understanding why God opened that door for me, but I know it helped me to starve my flesh and allow my spirit to reign.

Don't you realize that in a race everyone runs, but only one person gets the prize? So run to win! All athletes are disciplined in their training. They do it to win a prize that will fade away, but we do it for an eternal prize. **So I run with purpose in every step.** I am not just shadowboxing. **I discipline my body like an athlete, training it to do what it should.** Otherwise, I fear that after preaching to others I myself might be disqualified. (1 Corinthians 9:24-27)

Practice these principles on a day to day basis, training your flesh to obey the Spirit, so God can lead your life to His purpose for you! Run your race of faith to win! Don't stay seated on the sidelines. There is so much more action out on the field. If God tells you to jump, then jump—even if it scares you! There are gifts, talents, and abilities within you that you don't know are there. God knows they're there, and sometimes He has to mine them out of you like gold. Layers below a lifetime of fear, pride, shame, and anxiety is a beautiful, brightly shining child of God full of purpose and potential that will give God glory for all eternity! God knows how to gently and safely mine the treasure He's placed within you, and train the athlete of your inner man.

> **God knows how to gently and safely mine the treasure He's placed within you, and train the athlete of your inner man.**

Second Timothy 2:3-7 (NKJV) says,

You therefore must **endure hardship as a good soldier of Jesus Christ.** No one engaged in warfare entangles himself with the affairs of this life, that he may please him who enlisted him as a soldier. And also **if anyone competes in athletics, he is not crowned unless he competes according to the rules. The hardworking farmer must be first to partake of the crops.** Consider what I say, and may the Lord give you understanding in all things.

When you gave your life to Jesus, you became a child of God, yes. But you also received a job title that contains many descriptions. You are a soldier, an athlete, and a farmer. Fight and discipline yourself like a soldier, train and compete like an athlete, and work hard like a farmer! You are a workman for Jesus that will not be ashamed when He appears again, and you will receive a great reward. While you are on this earth, make the most of your time here, fight for the prize, run your race, and finish your course with victory.

> I have fought the good fight, I have finished the race, and I have remained faithful. (2 Timothy 4:7)

Your life becomes ruled by the Spirit as you walk in relationship and reliance on the Spirit of God every moment of the day. Acknowledging the truth of who you are in the spirit and resisting your flesh will strengthen your life from the inside out. As you obey the leadings of the Holy Spirit, He will lead you to a life full of the life of God, and you are transformed by His presence within you.

The Holy Spirit is always leading you to the life of God. The more that you obey the leadings of the Holy Spirit, the more your life will be transformed. Your whole self (spirit, soul, and body) becomes supernaturally charged by the power of God and you experience life more abundantly. This is how God intended for you to live at all times, ruled by the spirit, yet living in complete freedom.

Those who live only to satisfy their own sinful nature will harvest decay and death from that sinful nature. But those who live to please the Spirit will harvest everlasting life from the Spirit. So let's not get tired of doing what is good. At just the right time we will reap a harvest of blessing if we don't give up. (Galatians 6:8-9)

# Transform Your Life
## Application of Chapter Concepts

### A Moment of Reflection: Charge Yourself Up by Plugging into His Presence

1. Do you see an area of your life that could benefit from a spiritual adjustment?
   - If so, wake up your spirit man and fight! Stand up right now, begin to pray in tongues, and ask Holy Spirit to help you take control of your life again. Cause your spirit to rule over your flesh!

2. Think about how you've lived your life in the past, and how you want to live your life in the future.
   - How have you given in to the lusts of the flesh?
   - Now, forget the past, forgive yourself and others, and press toward the future! How would you like to start living life by the Spirit?

3. How do you imagine this could transform your life by obeying the Holy Spirit's leadings?
    - Have you noticed Holy Spirit leading you in the past?
    - Moving forward, in what ways do you feel led to feed your spirit?

4. When He leads you, remember to rely on Him and His love. He is the only One that can strengthen you to accomplish His will.

5. Create an atmosphere where you can read and hear God's Word, pray in tongues, and proclaim God's truth over your life.
    - In what other ways would you like to cultivate an atmosphere of Gods' presence in your home? With your friends and family?

6. Take some time to be quiet. Close your eyes. Imagine yourself in the future, and look at who you are in the spirit. A life that is yielded to God and led by His Spirit.
    - What do you see?

7. Spend time alone with God, and let Him guide your heart. What is the next step of faith that you can take in these areas? What do you sense He is leading you to do next? Listen to His voice, and write down thoughts that come to your mind. Remember, God's voice will always agree with the Word. If a thought comes that contradicts God's Word, you can replace it with the truth.

## My Transformation Scripture

What is a scripture that speaks to you about your life being ruled by the Spirit? Here are several suggestions:

- But if the Spirit of Him who raised Jesus from the dead dwells in you, He who raised Christ from the dead will also give life to your mortal bodies through His Spirit who dwells in you. (Romans 8:11 NKJV)
- So I say, let the Holy Spirit guide your lives. Then you won't be doing what your sinful nature craves. (Galatians 5:16)
- But the Holy Spirit produces this kind of fruit in our lives: love, joy, peace, patience, kindness, goodness, faithfulness, gentleness, and self-control. There is no law against these things! Those who belong to Christ Jesus have nailed the passions and desires of their

sinful nature to his cross and crucified them there. (Galatians 5:22-24)

- The Spirit alone gives eternal life. Human effort accomplishes nothing. And the very words I have spoken to you are spirit and life. (John 6:63)
- Keep watch and pray, so that you will not give in to temptation. For the spirit is willing, but the body is weak! (Matthew 26:41)
- And the Child grew and became strong in spirit, filled with wisdom; and the grace of God was upon Him. (Luke 2:40 NKJV)
- And Jesus Christ was revealed as God's Son by his baptism in water and by shedding his blood on the cross—not by water only, but by water and blood. And the Spirit, who is truth, confirms it with his testimony. So we have these three witnesses—the Spirit, the water, and the blood—and all three agree. (1 John 5:6-7)
- We know that whoever is born of God does not sin; but he who has been born of God keeps himself, and the wicked one does not touch him. (1 John 5:18 NKJV)

Write the scripture that you chose in your journal. Meditate on this verse throughout the day, and surround yourself with His presence.

### Time in His Presence

Spend some time with God meditating on your transformation scripture. What do you think the Lord is speaking to you through this verse?

### Life Application

Ask Holy Spirit to help you apply this scripture to your daily life. How can I apply this to my life today?

### Prayer

If you acknowledge that the Spirit of God in you is able to lead you and strengthen you so that you are not led by your flesh, but by His Spirit, then please pray with me:

*Lord, thank You for giving me Your Spirit, so that I can know You, have relationship with You, and be led by You in everything that I do. I know that You are always leading me to relationship with You, to Your best for my life, and to Your purpose for my life. Help me to be led by Your Spirit, not by my flesh. I invite You and ask for Your leadership and wisdom in every area of my life. Help me to not quench the Holy Spirit, but obey His drawings through Your ability, not mine. Thank you for showing me how to cultivate an atmosphere of Your presence in my home. I praise You and give You glory, God! In Jesus' name. Amen.*

# Chapter 12

## Results That Last a Lifetime!

Relying on God's Grace for Everything You Need

*May God give you more and more grace and peace as you grow in your knowledge of God and Jesus our Lord. By his divine power, God has given us everything we need for living a godly life. We have received all of this by coming to know him, the one who called us to himself by means of his marvelous glory and excellence.*
—2 Peter 1:2-3

Ever since I began applying the Word of God to my life on a daily basis, I have continued to see my life get better and better. I don't mean that in a bragging way. It's nothing that I've done well or even right. It's all because of my relationship with God and His grace working in my life.

This is what the Word of God promises us! That our lives will shine brighter and brighter, that His blessings will overtake us, and that we will overcome the world through our faith. Our faith is the victory that overcomes this fallen world that we live in because that is God's grace, His goodness towards us. Our part is to believe. His part is to do everything else. Sometimes, it's hard not to "do" in order to receive from God. It's a constant, daily practice for me to stay in a place of trust, rest, and reliance on God...a place of just believing, and not trying to help God get stuff done. Through faith, we receive the blessings of God's grace, all of His promises, and all of His ability working on our behalf.

Your life doesn't have to be up one day, and down the next day. You can consistently walk in joy, healing, financial prosperity, peaceful relationships, and emotional security. You can live in a place of constant wholeness in your spirit, soul, and body for the rest of your life!

Is that something that you desire? I sure hope you do, because that's what Jesus paid for you to experience each and every day of your life. If you want results that last a lifetime, then how do you get them? Let's find out!

## Perfectly Imperfect

In this lifetime, I have fallen short too many times to count. To this day, I fall short of the potential of Christ in me. On a daily basis I miss the mark, whether through sin, wrong thinking, unbelief, a lack of trust, unforgiveness, a wrong heart attitude, griping and complaining...all of these things are a stench in the nostrils of God, yet He loves me and continues to love me perfectly. I may not understand the Bible perfectly, and I don't have all the answers. I won't be perfect and I'm going to do things incorrectly. I'm ok with all of that, because I know my heart will be in the right place, nestled next to Him, and I will continue to do the best I can through His power working in me. Jesus was perfect for me.

Despite how much I fail, I've decided to live the rest of my life glorifying the One that saved me from a life of sin, bondage, and captivity. I will live my life to tell others of the hope, the calling, and the redemption that faith in

Jesus Christ offers. Living my life for Jesus is the best decision I've ever made. It's a daily choice of making Him a priority in my life, surrendering everything to Him, and obeying His every direction by His grace. When I began to live life *from* my relationship with God, instead of *for* my relationship with God, I experienced an entirely *new level of freedom.* Instead of trying to do for God, I learned how to live from God and it empowered me with His fullness on the inside. In fact, I experienced the power of my *new identity in Christ,* and I discovered my destiny. For me, this was the last step that put all the pieces of my spiritual puzzle together.

## His Ability versus My Ability

It can be very easy to switch back and forth between "doing" in order to receive something from God, to "doing" from relationship with God. Whenever we switch from *doing to receive something* to *doing from relationship,* then we will experience some sort of inner whiplash. I call this, His ability versus my ability. For me, I know when I'm *doing to receive* because I leave a place of peace in my heart. I get tired, discouraged, I lose hope, and sometimes I even want to give up. I get emotional and cry. Well, that means that I have gotten my eyes off of God and reliance upon Him, and my eyes are on myself and my performance. I'm trying to accomplish things in my own ability and strength in order to receive the results that I want. If I were to put this into words, it might sound like this: "I've got to get this done! I need to hurry up and do this so I can get this ____. I want to do this so I can have this ____." Versus, when God tells me to do something, I have grace for it. Maybe it stems from a desire in my heart, or a goal that God helped me set, or a verse in the Bible that I want to apply to my life. This might sound like: "God, will you help me to accomplish this today? Whatever we get done together is ok with me. I put the results in your hands and I commit this to you." The second scenario is *doing from a place of relationship and trust,* which is where we should always reside. That is how we stay in God's grace, and remain in a place of peace and joy while we are "getting things done" with God.

> Yes, I am the vine; you are the branches. Those who remain in me, and I in them, will produce much fruit. For apart from me you can do nothing. (John 15:5)

Apart from our relationship with God we can't do anything! From relationship with God, we can accomplish anything that God has placed within our hearts. What do I mean by that? Well, God places desires within your heart, and He uses those desires and passions to lead your life (Psalm 37:4). For example, I was very passionate about being healthy in my spirit, soul, and body. So, I pursued a job as a fitness trainer to help others reach their health and fitness goals. God has used that desire in my heart to give me training and experience so I can bless other people through those skill sets. God used the desires and passions within my heart to bring forth His purpose for my life. And He is doing the same thing in your life!

## Your Purpose in the Great Commission

What are you passionate about? What desires are in your heart today? If you're not sure yet, don't worry. After I got sober, it took time for me to discover what I was passionate about. At first, I was just led by the things that I knew *I didn't want to do.* I knew that I didn't want to be a drug addict anymore, and I didn't want to make decisions that would harm my life. I didn't want to be around people who cussed, cursed God, and lived a sinful life. I knew that I wanted to start making decisions that blessed my life and the people around me.

For many years, those two things helped me make decisions that greatly changed my life, until I could discern the desires in my heart. My *Walking in the New You! Workbook* is designed to help you discover God's purpose for your life, and create a life plan to help you pursue the desires and passions He has placed in your heart. This workbook is a great next step for pursuing God's purpose for your life!

Sometimes we can over-spiritualize things and look at our desires, our emotions, and our internal human responses as evil because they're natural. As I mentioned before, God made you to be you! God created you to have your desires, strengths, and passions so that He can use them in His kingdom. There is no one else like you in all of creation. You are special, unique, and one of a kind! The body of Christ needs you, and we need your passions and skill sets! Your DNA is uniquely and strategically knit together to build up and join together all the members of the body of Christ. If you're not doing what God's called you to do, then we (the body of Christ) are missing out! You are a vital member and asset in the church! We need each member of the body whole, knit together in unity, and walking in their purpose for the body of Christ to truly fulfill Jesus' Great Commission:

Jesus came and told his disciples, "I have been given all authority in heaven and on earth. Therefore, go and make disciples of all the nations, baptizing them in the name of the Father and the Son and the Holy Spirit. Teach these new disciples to obey all the commands I have given you. And be sure of this: I am with you always, even to the end of the age." (Matthew 28:18-20)

---

**God created you to have your desires, strengths, and passions so that He can use them in His kingdom.**

---

You have a part to play in God's kingdom. The body of Christ needs you! Look at the way Paul describes this in the book of Ephesians.

> Now these are the gifts Christ gave to the church: the apostles, the prophets, the evangelists, and the pastors and teachers. Their responsibility is to equip God's people to do his work and build up the church, the body of Christ. **This will continue until we all come to such unity in our faith and knowledge of God's Son that we will be mature in the Lord,**

**measuring up to the full and complete standard of Christ.** Then we will no longer be immature like children. We won't be tossed and blown about by every wind of new teaching. We will not be influenced when people try to trick us with lies so clever they sound like the truth. Instead, we will **speak the truth in love, growing in every way more and more like Christ, who is the head of his body, the church. He makes the whole body fit together perfectly. As each part does its own special work, it helps the other parts grow, so that the whole body is healthy and growing and full of love.**
(Ephesians 4:11-16)

As Christ's body, each one of us must value His Word and His instruction to the disciples, because we are His disciples on the earth today. Our proper knowledge and understanding of the Bible is essential to fulfilling the Great Commission, and building up the body of Christ, so that we can mature and bring forth God's kingdom on the earth.

God has a specific purpose for your life that will bring forth His kingdom of heaven on earth, and help the other members of the body...until the whole body is healthy, growing, and full of love. Will you help God, and pursue His purpose for your life today? If you feel like this is too big, or too great of a calling for your life, then you're right where you're supposed to be. God isn't asking you to do it on your own. He is asking you to do it through reliance upon Him and your relationship with Him. He is right here with you, and His grace is sufficient to help you accomplish it.

## Growing in Knowledge

Anytime that I've discussed God's love, blessing, goodness, faithfulness, strength, or power in the believer's life, it's all accomplished by the grace of God. God's grace is what enables you to do anything in the Christian life. It's what saved you and keeps you saved. God's grace empowers you to live the Christian life; it helps you, protects you, provides for you, balances you, enables you, and influences you with His goodness, ability, wisdom, favor, and blessing in every area of your life. There are so many beautiful things about God's grace that we could talk about, but I'm only going to cover a few. I encourage you to look into more scriptures on God's grace during your study time with the Lord, so that you can discover the depths of God's grace!

Did you know that you can receive *more* of God's grace working on your behalf? The Bible says that grace and peace is multiplied to you in the knowledge of God and in Jesus our Lord (2 Pet. 1:2). Growing in your knowledge of God and Jesus Christ will cause you to receive more grace in your life. What is the result of *more grace?* It would be more of God's divine strength, provision, ability, and power working in your life. Why do you receive more grace and peace as you grow in knowledge? Because God is the *God of all grace* (1 Pet. 5:10). God's nature and character is grace: it's His unconditional goodwill towards you and His divine ability to bring forth His perfect plan in your life. This is good news!

> **God's nature and character is grace: it's His unconditional goodwill towards you and His divine ability to bring forth His perfect plan in your life.**

As we grow in the knowledge of God, then we will understand Him more. From this understanding, we can model our lives after Him. Just because I love God doesn't mean that I've always modeled my life after Him. I've loved God for as long as I can remember, even when I was a drug addict. But I lacked the *knowledge* that I needed to live my life in a way that glorified Him. As a young child, I would lie in bed at night and pray, "God, make me more like you." Even though I fell away from Him as an adult, God saw my heart to live for Him and He hasn't given up on me since. He heard that young girl's prayer and marked me for His kingdom, "She's mine." One day, I'll understand fully how much God saved me from, and how much He empowered me to overcome...all the ways, all the things that God did to get me to where I'm at today. That is God's grace working in my life. Despite my mistakes, He made a way to bring me back to His perfect plan for my life. God is doing the same thing for you. Despite your mistakes, God is making a way for you and bringing His perfect plan to pass in your life.

> **Despite your mistakes, God is making a way for you and bringing His perfect plan to pass in your life.**

Whenever we intentionally shape our hearts, our minds, our actions, our words, and our will to match God's will, then we are becoming more like God. Every time that we discover another facet of God's nature and character, *we know more about Him.* Anytime that we apply His knowledge and divine wisdom to our life, *we become more like Him.* When we become more like God, our lives are filled with

Him! He *becomes us* and *we become Him*—we mirror Him in the things that we do, and our lives become a reflection of the Almighty God. Supernaturally, we reflect the God of all grace, and His grace overflows, fills, and empowers our life. We become the streams of living water that fill this earth with the presence, will, and aroma of God.

## The Beauty of Humility

Another way that we can walk in *more grace* is through *humility*. The Bible says that God resists the proud but *He gives grace to the humble* (1 Pet. 5:5). What does it mean to be humble? Personally, I think it means to agree with God about everything. If God says He created me for a purpose, then I can agree with Him. If God says that I am beautifully and wonderfully made, then I can agree with Him. The opposite of humility is pride; rejecting God and disagreeing with Him. If you want to live a life full of God's grace, then reject the way of pride and commit yourself to God's way! I love these scriptures from Proverbs that talk about pride versus a life committed to God in humility.

The path of the virtuous leads away from evil; whoever follows that path is safe. Pride goes before destruction, and haughtiness before a fall. Better to live humbly with the poor than to share plunder with the proud. Those who listen to instruction will prosper; those who trust the LORD will be joyful. The wise are known for their understanding, and pleasant words are persuasive. Discretion is a life-giving fountain to those who possess it, but discipline is wasted on fools. (Proverbs 16:17-22)

When pride comes, then comes disgrace, but with the humble is wisdom. (Proverbs 11:2)

The Bible makes it clear that blessings follow the humble, but disgrace follows the proud. This leads to the question: how do we humble ourselves and resist pride? By growing in the knowledge of God so we can agree with Him, and disagree with anything that goes against His will. I haven't done this perfectly, but my relationship with God has guided me in the right direction. I've made my relationship with God the most important thing in my life. Therefore, I prioritize Him above anything else. If God tells me to do something, I'm going to do it. If someone asks me to do something that disagrees with God's Word, then I'm not going to do it. God has defined His will, His nature, His character, and His plans for us in His Word. If we will submit to His Word and model our lives after Him, then we will receive more of His supernatural power, blessing, and ability working in our lives: God's grace! A person who adorns their life with the virtue of humility is so valuable and precious in the sight of God.

> You should clothe yourselves instead with the beauty that comes from within, the unfading beauty of a gentle and quiet spirit, which is so precious to God. (1 Peter 3:4)

## Resist the Devil

The Bible also tells us that we receive more grace not only when we submit to God, but when we *resist the devil.*

> But he gives *more grace.* Therefore it says, *"God opposes the proud but gives grace to the humble." Submit yourselves* therefore to God. *Resist the devil,* and he will flee from you. (James 4:6-7 ESV)

You are operating in humility when you submit to God and resist the devil, and then the devil flees from you! Have you ever experienced a situation in your life where you knew that you were facing a demonic attack? Or, you were facing a situation and you knew that it wasn't God's will for you to be facing that? Maybe it was some type of sickness, a natural disaster, temptation, or some type of suffering. These are just a handful of things that you may face in this lifetime because this world has fallen to sin. Until you get to heaven, you're not going to have perfect circumstances in life. This is part of the importance of growing in the knowledge of God, so that when these things come against you, you understand that they aren't God's will for you, and you can resist them! When you actively resist these types of negative situations, you are enforcing God's will for you.

> **When you actively resist these types of negative situations, you are enforcing God's will for you.**

This is an elemental part of walking in *your new identity* in Christ, and fulfilling God's purpose for your life. As you do this, you will grow in spiritual maturity, become more rooted in your identity, and you will have a thorough understanding of how to apply God's Word to your life. You will have so many testimonies, saying, "I believed this verse, resisted this situation, and now I'm seeing victory in this area of my life!" Don't be afraid of your testimonies, the areas that you've overcome, or places where you've fallen short. Other people need to hear your testimony, how you've overcome, and what God's done in your life!

> And they have conquered him by the blood of the Lamb and by the word of their testimony, for they loved not their lives even unto death.
> (Revelation 12:11 ESV)

Sharing your testimony is how you give God glory, and it's another way to overcome and resist the enemy. When the time is right, go and tell the world what God did for you. Tell the world how God loved you, transformed your life, gave you purpose, and set you free. Praise God! You can share your testimonies of what God's doing in your life at NewYouMinistries.com/testimony.

# Receiving More of God's Power

Receiving more of God's grace in my life is definitely something that I want, and I hope you do too! Here are several ways to receive *more grace* (God's supernatural ability and provision) in your life:

- Grow in your knowledge of God through a daily commitment to Him and His Word
- Walk in humility by
    - Agreeing with God and submitting to His will.
    - Rejecting the prideful way.
    - Resisting the devil.
    - Counter situations that don't align with God's will for you.

The Bible puts all of these things together for us in 1 Peter 5:6-10 ESV:

**Humble yourselves,** therefore, under the mighty hand of God so that at the proper time he may exalt you, casting all your anxieties on him, because he cares for you. Be sober-minded; be watchful. Your adversary the devil prowls around like a roaring lion, seeking someone to devour. **Resist him,** firm in your faith, knowing that the same kinds of suffering are being experienced by your brotherhood throughout the world. And after you have suffered a little while, **the God of all grace, who has called you to his eternal glory in Christ, will himself restore, confirm, strengthen, and establish you.**

When you rely on the God of all grace for everything you need, your life will be empowered from the inside out, and you will be filled with God's strength, power, and blessing. As my spiritual father of the faith says,

*God will make you look good!*
– Andrew Wommack

Despite your inability, imperfection, and mistakes, God's grace will continually adorn your life with His goodness. God will make you look good even when you mess up! All God needs from me is a "yes" in my heart, small steps of faith, and the results are up to Him.

# It All Starts and Ends Here

If you want results that last a lifetime, whether it's setting and accomplishing goals, pursuing your greatest passion, or accomplishing God's purpose for your life, it all starts and ends with a relationship with God. It's never about how much you accomplish for God, or doing everything perfectly along the way. Trust me, I'm preaching to the choir here. I have to remind myself of these things constantly. Just yesterday, I was encouraging myself in the Lord like David did; reminding myself to keep believing and run towards my giant instead of away from him. With God, I can do anything. Without God, I can do nothing.

Whether I'm working out, setting goals, going to a meeting at work, or trying to manage my time more effectively, I am constantly asking God for help. Constantly. Most of the time, I don't feel like working out, being a leader, cooking healthy meals, or pursuing my purpose. But, every day I wake up with God on my mind, and I devote the first part of my day to be with Him. I get filled up with God, and He puts His desires, His passions, His strength, and His purpose in my heart. I have no other desire but to be like Him, and I automatically end up accomplishing all of these things because He's first. God flows out of me because I spend time looking at Him, learning from Him, and listening to Him. By default, I have strength to workout, eat healthy, maintain routines, set healthy habits, and accomplish goals. I do what He tells me to do and I ask Him for help every step of the way.

I'm sure I'm not the only one who wears a lot of hats, or carries a lot of responsibilities. Take a moment to think about who you are, and who the people around you expect you to be. Are you a wife? A mother? A friend? A daughter? An employee? A sister? A boss? A leader? A church member? Some of you are saying yes to each one of those things. Whether you are or not, I know that I can't fulfill one title on that list without God's divine help and support. I need God's grace to accomplish anything in this world, and I can only do it by staying connected to the Vine, through an intimate, daily relationship with Him.

> If you abide in me, and my words abide in you, ask whatever you wish, and it will be done for you. By this my Father is glorified, that you bear much fruit and so prove to be my disciples. As the Father has loved me, so have I loved you. Abide in my love. If you keep my commandments, you will abide in my love, just as I have kept my Father's commandments

and abide in his love. These things I have spoken to you, that my joy may be in you, and that your joy may be full. (John 15:7-11 ESV)

The only way we can live the victorious Christian life is through relationship with God. We are all human, and not one of us is perfect. God isn't asking us to be perfect, He's asking us to believe in Him and remain connected to Him. The only way we can do that is through an intimate, loving relationship with our Creator. The more that I know Him and experience His love working in me, the more I'll be able to trust Him when He asks me to talk in front of a live camera, or write a book that encourages others, or rely on Him to finish something that He's asked me to start. The results aren't up to me or you; they're up to Him. All that I have to do is show up and trust Him, even if I do it scared and shaking in my boots. He is faithful to use what I give to Him: completely imperfect yet perfectly in love with Him.

## God is Our Helper

When you rely on God's grace for everything you need, you will receive results that last a lifetime. No more being up one day and down the next day. You will be strong in your inner man because of your relationship with God, and through Him, you will have the divine ability of God to accomplish the impossible in your life. *What used to be impossible for you will become the testimony of victory in your life!*

In closing, I'd like to encourage you with these verses:

> May grace and peace be multiplied to you in the knowledge of God and of Jesus our Lord. **His divine power has granted to us all things that pertain to life and godliness, through the knowledge of him** who called us to his own glory and excellence, **by which he has granted to us his precious and very great promises, so that through them you may become partakers of the divine nature**, having escaped from the corruption that is in the world because of sinful desire. For this very reason, *make every effort to supplement your faith with virtue, and virtue with knowledge, and knowledge with self-control, and self-control with steadfastness, and steadfastness with godliness, and godliness with brotherly affection, and brotherly affection with love.* **For if these qualities are yours and are increasing, they keep you from being ineffective or unfruitful in the knowledge of our Lord Jesus Christ.** For whoever lacks these qualities is so nearsighted that he is blind, having forgotten

that he was cleansed from his former sins. Therefore, brothers, **be all the more diligent to confirm your calling and election, for if you practice these qualities you will never fall.** For in this way there will be richly provided for you an entrance into the eternal kingdom of our Lord and Savior Jesus Christ. (2 Peter 1:2-11 ESV)

God's Word is working in your heart, bringing forth the divine nature and promises of God in your life. Through the continual practice of applying this knowledge to your life, you will grow in the attributes of godliness. These spiritual principles will further help you to abide in Christ, causing you to live an effective and fruitful life!

Growing in the knowledge of God will cause grace and peace to be multiplied in your life, and you will overflow with the blessings of God increasingly over time. Every day you will look more like God; a living reflection of God proving His perfect will in your life. This daily walk will sharpen you, build your character, and bring you success.

Maybe this is too hard for you to believe right now, but you still have hope for it in your heart. Maybe you desire these things, you want to believe them and see a change in your life, but this all seems too good to be true.

Well, the gospel of Jesus Christ is too good to be true. No one deserves it, but Jesus paid for you to receive it. By only believing, you can receive God's precious promises and amazing purpose for your life. That's His grace towards you. Your past cannot ruin, cancel, or lessen God's great purpose for your life. In fact, God's love and grace are so good, that He will even cause the bad things in your past to complement His perfect plans for your life. He will so completely and perfectly restore and redeem every area of your life that you won't even recognize your past self. You will shine with His goodness and glory!

> But whenever someone turns to the Lord, the veil is taken away. For the Lord is the Spirit, and wherever the Spirit of the Lord is, there is freedom. So all of us who have had that veil removed can see and reflect the glory of the Lord. And the Lord—who is the Spirit—makes us more and more like him as we are changed into his glorious image. (2 Cor. 3:16-18)

Precious child of God, you are loved, and your Heavenly Father is fighting for you. He is working behind the scenes to bring forth His perfect plan for your life. Now is your time to arise and shine. You are called for such a time as this, and you will accomplish great things with God.

Join with me and tell the nations how good our God is.

*Thank you for letting me be a part of your journey. I'm praying for you as you walk in your new identity. Welcome to the life of your dreams! Love, Erin*

# Transform Your Life

## Application of Chapter Concepts

### A Moment of Reflection: Time for *New You* Transformation!

1. Have you allowed the voice of your past or any imperfections to rule the decision you make?
   - If so, how are you going to take a stand against those things today?
   - How are you going to prioritize what God says about you, about your future, and about His purpose for your life?
   - Now, let God's grace (His power, ability, and provision) bring forth those promises. Press into your relationship with God, and focus on Him.

2. Spend time alone with God, and let Him guide your heart. What is the next step of faith that you can take in these areas? What do you sense He is leading you to do next? Listen to His voice, and write down

thoughts that come to your mind. Remember, God's voice will always agree with the Word. If a thought comes that contradicts God's Word, you can replace it with the truth.

## My Transformation Scripture

What is a scripture that speaks to you about relying on God's grace for everything you need? Here are several suggestions:

- Through him we have also obtained access by faith into this grace in which we stand, and we rejoice in hope of the glory of God. (Romans 5:2 ESV)
- In view of all this, make every effort to respond to God's promises. Supplement your faith with a generous provision of moral excellence, and moral excellence with knowledge, and knowledge with self-control, and self-control with patient endurance, and patient endurance with godliness, and godliness with brotherly affection, and brotherly affection with love for everyone. The more you grow like this, the more productive and useful you will be in your knowledge of our Lord Jesus Christ. (2 Peter 1:5-8)

- I don't mean to say that I have already achieved these things or that I have already reached perfection. But I press on to possess that perfection for which Christ Jesus first possessed me. No, dear brothers and sisters, I have not achieved it, but I focus on this one thing: Forgetting the past and looking forward to what lies ahead, I press on to reach the end of the race and receive the heavenly prize for which God, through Christ Jesus, is calling us. (Philippians 3:12-1)
- Taste and see that the LORD is good. Oh, the joys of those who take refuge in him! Fear the LORD, you his godly people, for those who fear him will have all they need. Even strong young lions sometimes go hungry, but those who trust in the LORD will lack no good thing. (Psalm 34:8-10)
- If you keep yourself pure, you will be a special utensil for honorable use. Your life will be clean, and you will be ready for the Master to use you for every good work. Run from anything that stimulates youthful lusts. Instead, pursue righteous living, faithfulness, love, and peace. Enjoy the companionship of those who call on the Lord with pure hearts.
(2 Timothy 2:21-22)

- But my life is worth nothing to me unless I use it for finishing the work assigned me by the Lord Jesus—the work of telling others the Good News about the wonderful grace of God. (Acts 20:24)

Write the scripture that you chose in your journal. Meditate on this verse throughout the day, and remind yourself of God's perfect plan for your life.

## Time in His Presence

Spend some time with God meditating on your transformation scripture. What do you think the Lord is speaking to you through this verse?

## Life Application

Ask Holy Spirit to help you apply this scripture to your daily life. How can I apply this to my life today?

## Prayer

If you are ready to walk according to God's will for the rest of your life, and commit every area of your heart to Him today, then please pray with me:

*Lord, thank You for Jesus! Thank You for equipping me with the power of Jesus Christ in me. I am ready to rely on You for everything that I need. Help me with the areas that have seemed impossible, and make them a testimony of victory in my life! Give me courage and boldness to accomplish my purpose on the earth. Thank You for strengthening me, establishing me, perfecting me, and bringing stability to my life for Your glory on earth and in heaven. You are Lord of my life! To God and Jesus Christ be all the glory now and forever. In Jesus' name I pray. Amen.*

## Seeking a Christ-Centered Community as You Walk in Your New Identity?

Please don't do life alone! Join Erin and our online community of women who are doing life together, trusting God together, and pursuing their purpose together! Come and join us at **NewYouMinistries.com**!

While you're there, subscribe to Erin's newsletter for daily tips and encouragement, and follow her on YouTube, Facebook, and Instagram at @erinweisbrodt.

To help you discover and pursue God's purpose for your life, Erin has created the *Walking in the New You! Workbook*, the *Hello, New You! Productivity Planner*, and *Journey of Faith: A Daily Prayer Journal*, so that you can practice the principles she shared throughout this book. These valuable resources were designed to help you develop your relationship with the Lord, deepen your understanding of the Bible, and help you to apply its life-altering wisdom to every area of your life. To order these resources, visit Erin's website, **NewYouMinistries.com**.

## Appendix A

# Receiving Jesus

Making Jesus the Lord and Savior of your life will transform your life forever. This is the most important decision you will ever make!

The Bible says in Romans 10:9-10, "If you openly declare that Jesus is Lord and believe in your heart that God raised him from the dead, you will be saved. For it is by believing in your heart that you are made right with God, and it is by openly declaring your faith that you are saved."

Because of Jesus Christ, your sins have been forgiven for all time, and you can live in relationship with God now, and in heaven for all eternity. All that you have to do is believe this in your heart and declare it with your mouth. This is how you receive Jesus as the Lord and Savior of your life.

Pray out loud, *"Jesus, I believe that You are the Son of God; that You took my sins, died for me, and rose from the dead. I confess that You are my Lord and Savior. Thank you for saving me!"*

Now, in your spirit, you are identical to Jesus Christ, and you have become born-again. You are brand new in Christ, and ready to walk out your new identity in Him. *Hello, New You!*

# Appendix B

# Receiving the Holy Spirit

When you receive the baptism of the Holy Spirit, your life is filled with the power of God, so that you can live this new life with supernatural results. The Holy Spirit in you is how God helps you, equips you, and leads you through your life in victory.

Luke 11:10, 13 says, "For everyone who asks, receives. Everyone who seeks, finds. And to everyone who knocks, the door will be opened...how much more will your heavenly Father give the Holy Spirit to those who ask him." When you believe God and ask Him to fill you with the Holy Spirit, you receive!

Pray, *"Father, I surrender to you completely. I ask you to baptize me with your Holy Spirit with the evidence of speaking in tongues. Thank you for filling me with the power that enables me to live the victorious Christian life. By faith I receive it now in Jesus' name."*

Congratulations! I encourage you to welcome this new part of your life with open arms and rejoicing! Give Him thanks for all that He has done for you and all that He is going to continue to do for you! I encourage you to open your mouth and speak in tongues immediately. This is a gift that God has given us as believers. It will truly help you, edify you, and give you the wisdom of God that you need to live the victorious Christian life.

Open your mouth and begin to make sounds that rise up from your heart. These sounds will be unrecognizable to your understanding. As you continue to speak them out loud with faith you will be praying the perfect prayer (1 Cor. 14:2), edifying yourself (1 Cor. 14:4), and building yourself up on your most holy faith (Jude 1:20). When you pray in tongues you are praying God's perfect will, giving thanks well, and receiving wisdom from God directly to our spirit. I encourage you to pray in tongues daily, so that you are receiving supernatural help from God.

Continue to ask Holy Spirit to help you in your day-to-day life, and rely on Him for everything you need. I'm rejoicing with you as you step into your new life!

# Endnotes

## Chapter 2

[1] "G4151 - pneuma - Strong's Greek Lexicon (kjv)." Blue Letter Bible. Accessed 31 Oct, 2023. https://www.blueletterbible.org/lexicon/g4151/kjv/tr/0-1/

[2] "G5590 - psychē - Strong's Greek Lexicon (kjv)." Blue Letter Bible. Accessed 31 Oct, 2023. https://www.blueletterbible.org/lexicon/g5590/kjv/tr/0-1/

[3] "G2137 - euodoō - Strong's Greek Lexicon (kjv)." Blue Letter Bible. Accessed 31 Oct, 2023. https://www.blueletterbible.org/lexicon/g2137/kjv/tr/0-1/

[4] "G4983 - sōma - Strong's Greek Lexicon (kjv)." Blue Letter Bible. Accessed 31 Oct, 2023. https://www.blueletterbible.org/lexicon/g4983/kjv/tr/0-1/

[5] "G4053 - perissos - Strong's Greek Lexicon (kjv)." Blue Letter Bible. Accessed 31 Oct, 2023. https://www.blueletterbible.org/lexicon/g4053/kjv/tr/0-1/

[6]"H7965 - šālôm - Strong's Hebrew Lexicon (kjv)." Blue Letter Bible. Accessed 1 Nov, 2023. https://www.blueletterbible.org/lexicon/h7965/kjv/wlc/0-1/

[7]"G3339 - metamorphoō - Strong's Greek Lexicon (kjv)." Blue Letter Bible. Accessed 1 Nov, 2023. https://www.blueletterbible.org/lexicon/g3339/kjv/tr/0-1/

[8]Harper Douglas, "Etymology of metamorphosis," Online Etymology Dictionary, accessed November 1, 2023, https://www.etymonline.com/word/metamorphosis.

[9] "Metamorphosis" definition – *The language data is provided by Oxford Languages, part of Oxford University Press*

[10]"G342 - anakainōsis - Strong's Greek Lexicon (KJV)." Blue Letter Bible. Accessed 1 Nov, 2023. https://www.blueletterbible.org/lexicon/g342/kjv/tr/0-1/

## Chapter 3

[1]"G1411 - dynamis - Strong's Greek Lexicon (kjv)." Blue Letter Bible. Accessed 1 Nov, 2023. https://www.blueletterbible.org/lexicon/g1411/kjv/tr/0-1/

## Chapter 6

[1] "G3640 - oligopistos - Strong's Greek Lexicon (kjv)." Blue Letter Bible. Accessed 1 Nov, 2023. https://www.blueletterbible.org/lexicon/g3640/kjv/tr/0-1/

[2] "Incredulous." Merriam-Webster.com Dictionary, Merriam-Webster, https://www.merriam-webster.com/dictionary/incredulous. Accessed 1 Nov. 2023.

## Chapter 8

[1] "H2377 - ḥāzôn - Strong's Hebrew Lexicon (kjv)." Blue Letter Bible. Accessed 1 Nov, 2023. https://www.blueletterbible.org/lexicon/h2377/kjv/wlc/0-1/

[2] Savelle Foy, Terri (2012). *Imagine Big: Unlock the Secret to Living Out Your Dreams.* Book. Gospel Light Publications, 2013. Print, https://www.terri.com/product/imagine-big/. Accessed November 14, 2023.

[3]Based on information from Medium Website in an article titled "Law of Attraction: History and Overview". https://medium.com/mind-altar/law-of-attraction-history-a-80bc52daa925

**Chapter 10**

[1]"G5485 - charis - Strong's Greek Lexicon (kjv)." Blue Letter Bible. Accessed 1 Nov, 2023. https://www.blueletterbible.org/lexicon/g5485/kjv/tr/0-1/

[2]"G4327 - prosdechomai - Strong's Greek Lexicon (kjv)." Blue Letter Bible. Accessed 2 Nov, 2023. https://www.blueletterbible.org/lexicon/g4327/kjv/tr/0-1/

[3]"H7673 - šāḇaṯ - Strong's Hebrew Lexicon (kjv)." Blue Letter Bible. Accessed 2 Nov, 2023. https://www.blueletterbible.org/lexicon/h7673/kjv/wlc/0-1/

# Additional Copyrights

Scripture quotations marked AMP are taken from the Amplified® Bible. Copyright © 2015 by The Lockman Foundation. Used by permission. www.lockman.org.

Scripture quotations marked AMPC were taken from the Amplified® Bible. Copyright © 1954, 1958, 1962, 1964, 1965, 1987 by The Lockman Foundation. Used by permission. www.lockman.org.

Scripture quotations are from The ESV® Bible (The Holy Bible, English Standard Version®), © 2001 by Crossway, a publishing ministry of Good News Publishers. Used by permission. All rights reserved.

Scripture quotations marked KJV are taken from The Holy Bible, King James Version®. Copyright © 1769 Cambridge Edition. King James Bible Online, 2023. www.kingjamesbibleonline.org.

Scripture quotations marked NASB and NASB95 have been taken from the New American Standard Bible®. Copyright © 1960, 1971, 1977, 1995, 2020 by The Lockman Foundation. Used by permission. All rights reserved. www.lockman.org.

Scripture quotations marked NKJV have been taken from the New King James Version®. Copyright © 1982 by Thomas Nelson. Used by permission. All rights reserved.

Scripture quotations marked NLT have been taken from the *Holy Bible*, New Living Translation. Copyright © 1996, 2004, 2015 by Tyndale House Foundation. Used by permission of Tyndale House Publishers, Inc., Carol Stream, Illinois 60188. All rights reserved.

Scripture quotations marked TPT are from The Passion Translation®. Copyright © 2017, 2018, 2020 by Passion & Fire Ministries, Inc. Used by permission. All rights reserved. ThePassionTranslation.com.

# Help Share God-Given Messages around the World!

This message was written and published through The Message Launch Program, an initiative supported by the "I have a Message" Foundation INC. (IHAM), a 501c3 organization.

To learn more about IHAM and discover how you can contribute to sharing messages like this globally, please visit: **IHAM.org**.

Blessings,

**Rigel and Jenna Drake-Garcia**

*Founders of the I Have a Message Foundation, INC., and MessageLaunchProgram.com*

# About the Author

Are you ready to fulfill your destiny and transform your life? Start relying on God's strength within you to *make new choices today!*

Erin Weisbrodt calls the picturesque Woodland Park, Colorado, her home along with her loving family. Erin's passion for healthy living and the beauty of nature often leads her to explore the stunning landscapes with her husband on hikes!

Erin's personal journey, a remarkable transformation ignited by the power of God working from within, has inspired her to write the book *Hello, New You!* With a heart full of hope, her deep connection with her current vibrant community of women, and a desire to empower women worldwide, Erin shares her story, offering a guiding light to those who dream of a life filled with purpose, joy, and divine transformation.

Consider this book your official invitation to God into every aspect of your life, allowing Him to free you from any limitations hindering your full potential. Grow in your faith and discover the divine plan ordained specifically for you.

Erin also wrote a follow-up of this book, *Walking in the New You! Workbook,* along with her *Hello, New You! Productivity Planner,* and *Prayer Journal.* You can learn more about these resources at **NewYouMinistries.com**.

If you would like to partner with us and help others around the world to fulfill their destiny and be transformed by relying on God's strength, you can learn more at **NewYouMinistries.com/give, or simply scan the QR code below!**